CONTENTS

FOREWORD

THE CURTAIN RISES

Through most of the last century, the world was widely perceived as divided into two realms separated by what British prime minister Winston Churchill once called the "iron curtain." This curtain was, of course, not really made of iron, but of ideas and values. Countries to the west of this symbolic curtain, including the United States, were democracies founded upon the economic principles of capitalism. To the east, in the Soviet Union, a new social and economic order known as communism prevailed. The United States and the Soviet Union were locked for much of the twentieth century in a struggle for military, economic, and political dominance around the world.

But the Soviet Union could not sustain its own weight, burdened as it was by a hugely inefficient centralized government bureaucracy, by long-term neglect of domestic needs in favor of spending untold billions on the military, and by the systematic repression of thought and expression among its citizens. For years the military and internal police apparatus had held together the Soviet Union's diverse peoples. But even these entities could not overcome the corruption, the inefficiency, and the inability of the Communist system to provide the basic necessities for the Soviet people.

The unrest that signaled the beginning of the end for the Soviet Union began in the satellite countries of Eastern Europe in 1988—in East Germany, followed by Hungary, and Poland. By 1990, the independence movement had moved closer to the Soviet heartland. Lithuania became the first Baltic nation to declare its independence. By December 1991, all fifteen union republics— Armenia, Azerbaijan, Belarus, Estonia, Georgia, Kazakhstan, Kyrgyzstan, Latvia, Lithuania, Moldova, Russia, Tajikistan, Turkmenistan, Ukraine, Uzbekistan—had done the same. The Soviet Union had officially ceased to exist.

Today the people of new nations such as Uzbekistan, Latvia, Belarus, Georgia, Ukraine, and Russia itself (still the largest nation on earth) must deal with the loss of the certainties of the Soviet era and face the new economic and social challenges of the present. The fact that many of these regions have little if any history of self-governance adds to the problem. For better or worse, many social problems were kept in check by a powerful government during the Soviet era, and long-standing cultural, ethnic, and other tensions are once again threatening to tear apart these new and fragile nations. Whether these regions make an effective transition to a market economy based on capitalism and resolves their internal economic crises by becoming vital and successful participants in world trade; whether their social crises push them back in the direction of dictatorship or civil war, or move them toward greater political, ethnic, and religious tolerance; and perhaps most important of all, whether average citizens can come to believe in their own ability to improve their lives and their own power to create a government and a nation of laws that works in their own best interests, are questions that the entire world, not just former Soviet citizens are pondering.

Sociologists and political scientists alike point to instability in the former Soviet republics as a serious threat to world peace and the balance of global power, and therefore it is more important than ever to be accurately informed about this politically and economically critical part of the world. With Modern Nations: Former Soviet Republics, Lucent Books provides information about the people and recent history of the former Soviet republics, with an emphasis on those aspects of their culture, history, and current situation that seem most likely to play a role in the future course of each of these new nations emerging from the shadows of the now vanished iron curtain.

INTRODUCTION

THE CHANGING GIANT

Russia is the largest country on earth, covering one-eighth of the world's land surface. It stretches east from the Baltic Sea across the northernmost stretches of Europe, through Central Asia, all the way to the western edge of the Pacific Ocean north of China. It reaches north into the Arctic Circle and spreads south to the Black Sea, the edge of the Middle East.

In the middle of the twentieth century it was even larger. Then called the Union of Soviet Socialist Republics (USSR), or Soviet Union, it included a number of now independent nations, such as Estonia and Kazakhstan, along its western and southwestern borders. Its shadow was larger still—European nations such as Poland, Czechoslovakia, and Hungary were under its control, and it supported Communist nations as far-flung as Cuba, Angola, and North Vietnam.

The physical size of Russia, known officially today either by that name or by the longer term Russian Federation, serves as an appropriate symbol for the nation's huge role in the history of the twentieth century. There were, historians agree, no events of greater world significance in the 1900s than the two major political upheavals in Russia. The first occurred near the beginning of the century, in 1917, when Vladimir Ulyanov, known as Lenin, and the Bolshevik Party established communism and formed the Soviet Union. The second happened near the end of the century, when the Soviet Union and communism itself crumbled under the weight of its own inefficiency, corruption, and lies. Still, momentous as these two events were in themselves, what happened in the years between has had the most profound effect on Russians and the world.

THE SOVIET ERA

To understand how dramatic an effect communism had on Russia, it is important to understand the basic philosophy of communism and how it differs from the philosophy of capitalism, practiced by most developed nations. Communists believe that society should be set up in a way that ensures that the basic needs of society as a whole such as food and a place to live, are met, rather than in a way that allows and even encourages individuals to strive for a better life. Capitalism, on the other hand, stresses personal responsibility for finding a job and for taking care of oneself and one's family. Under capitalism, people can spend their money as they choose, even if those around them are in need.

Communism still has many supporters both in Russia and around the world. Its adherents argue that the vast majority of the world's people struggle to stay alive and thus are better off under communism, where the entire society is organized around ensuring that everyone has food in their stomachs and a roof over their heads. Capitalism is pleasant for the economically successful, but it also results in huge discrepancies between rich and poor. In the Soviet Union, life was hard for almost everyone, but homeless people did not huddle in cold alleys, all children were fed to the best of their community's ability, and anyone capable of work had a job. Some Americans saw the collapse of communism as a

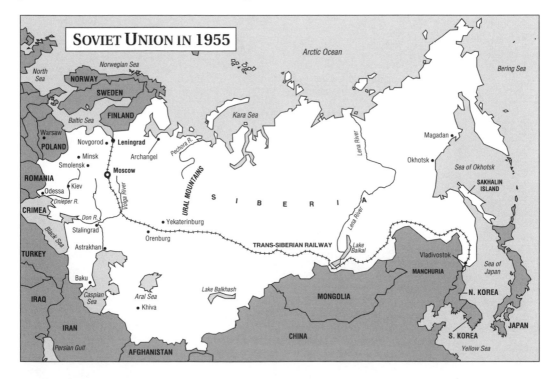

sign of the superiority of the American way of life, but according to noted historian Robert Service, those who wish to understand contemporary history must look deeper and not "assume that capitalism has all the answers to the problems faced by our troubled world." Communism in the Soviet Union may have failed but, according to Service, capitalism "has yet to succeed for most of the world's people most of the time."[1]

Communism failed in the Soviet Union not because it was wrong but because it was impractical. It turned out to be impossible to run a country based on the premise that every individual would put the good of the community above his or her own. People stopped working hard because there was no personal gain in doing so, and the economy began to crumble. Leaders did not in fact want to live like the average citizen. Their riches—and average citizens' resentment—grew. Frustrated and angered by what they perceived to be the resistance of the people, in the 1920s Communist leaders began exiling or executing those identified as self-centered or unsupportive of the Communist government. The workers' paradise Russia's leaders claimed they were creating slipped further out of reach as the century progressed.

Russian Communists march to mark the seventy-ninth anniversary of the Bolshevik Revolution.

THE NEW RUSSIA

The collapse of the Soviet Union in 1991 is seen by many Russians more as a failure of leadership than of the ideals of communism, and many Russians today regret losing what was good about communism in order to get rid of what was not. Nevertheless, by the 1980s it was obvious that communism was not working as planned. The question, however, was what kind of political and economic system would work better. That issue remains controversial, and the result has been growing chaos that threatens the stability of the entire federation.

The chaos in the government and economy of Russia today can be traced back to one core issue: power. Russians debate who should have power, and how much, and how it should be exercised, but there are no clear answers. The question of the allocation of power has made antagonists of the president and the Duma, the Russian parliament, each of whom seeks greater authority. This is unlikely to change in the foreseeable future. Another aspect of the struggle for political power in the new Russia involves ethnicity. The population of today's Russian Federation is now more than 80 percent ethnic Russian, higher than it has ever been, because many nonethnic Russian regions, such as Ukraine, are now independent countries. Still, many small ethnic groups remain, and want assurances they will not be swallowed up. The Russian Federation is divided into twenty-one autonomous republics and dozens of smaller regions, largely along ethnic lines, to satisfy non-Russians that their own cultures will have a home base in a country traditionally monopolized by ethnic Russians.

Because ethnic Russians and non-Russians traditionally have been adversaries, this division into ethnic republics has created some new problems. Some ethnic republics want to stay in the federation but govern themselves; others, such as Chechnya, want independence. The Russian Federation government is reluctant to give up as much central power as the ethnic republics demand, and Russia will fight to keep its present borders, as shown by the disastrous and brutal suppression in 1995 of the Chechen bid for independence, and the resumption of hostilities in 1999. Whether the Russian Federation will maintain its present shape and size remains to be seen, and how much freedom ethnic minorities will have to govern themselves are important issues in the power struggles today.

A third aspect of the struggle for power in today's Russia is economic. Communism operated with what is called a "command economy," which means in simplest terms that the government decided what products will be made, in what quantities, where, and by whom. In its opposite, a market economy, businesspeople make such decisions—what products or services to offer, how to market them, and what to charge based on expectations of profit. Thus in a command economy, the government has power over money and business, and in a market economy individuals do.

Generations of Russians lived with a government that had power over them and took responsibility for them. It provided them with a workplace, guaranteed continued employment, and, usually, housing. Today's Russians have no history of responsibility for their own lives. According to renowned political scientists Daniel Yergin and Thane Gustafson, "The Russian . . . family is unusually dependent on the workplace. It is absolutely critical to grasp this fact in order to understand the kind of challenges ahead."[2]

The government no longer has the power it once had, but it will take time for Russian citizens to understand how to fill the gap and take charge of their own lives. Most Russians have never had a bank account or written a check. Only recently did they begin having to find their own jobs. Russians who start businesses do not have the advantage of already established laws protecting and controlling business, or experience in such practices as negotiating binding contracts or collecting money owed. The missing pieces in former Soviet citizens' understanding of how a market economy works have thus created a number of problems. Without clear rules or common understanding, there is little chance that anyone can or will be punished for cheating or stealing, and organized crime and unethical individuals have been quick to take advantage of the situation.

AN UNCERTAIN FUTURE

Faced with skyrocketing crime rates and other woes such as inflation and unemployment, Russians, therefore, are deeply divided over whether the fall of communism was good or bad. A powerful Soviet military and police created oppression but also maintained order and reduced crime. The command economy at least ensured that basic needs were met. On the other hand,

many feel that Russia's problems are painful but temporary and must simply be weathered on the road to a democratic society. They feel the end result—greater personal freedom and prosperity—will be worth the present difficulties.

Those who wish to see a stable, functioning market economy take hold may be running out of time. The new Communist Party has been steadily gaining political support. A Communist, Gennady Zyuganov, would probably have been president in 1996 but for Yeltsin's last-minute media blitz to discredit the Communists. Many predict that Vladimir Putin will be unable to reverse this trend, which may allow the Communists to gain enough power to be able to change the country's constitution in whatever way they wish.

Russia today, in the words of one government minister, "does not change every year. It changes every month."[3] As the country's leaders struggle over power, ordinary people try to take charge of their lives, and the world waits and watches to see what role this giant will play in the twenty-first century.

A Chechen rebel looks over the rubble in Grozny, Chechnya, where the fight for independence from Russia has taken place.

1

Building Communism

For centuries there were essentially two kinds of Russians. The first group, the nobles, inherited and bequeathed fortunes and property. The second, vastly larger group, the peasants, barely had enough to survive. The nobles believed they were entitled to power over others and could use it however they wished—justly or unjustly, kindly or cruelly. The peasants, called serfs, believed they had no power, felt no entitlement to power, and simply endured whatever came their way. These two groups' views of themselves and each other—essentially views about power and privilege—help to explain twentieth-century Russian history and the way Russians think today.

The nineteenth-century Russian army serves as a good illustration of the society as a whole. On the bottom rung of the army hierarchy were the foot soldiers, whose service was donated without their permission by the nobles on whose land they worked. Their job was to storm the enemy in such numbers that at least a few of them would survive the barrage of bullets and cannons, force the enemy to scatter or retreat, and thus clear the way for the mounted troops to come in and secure the victory. Foot soldiers often charged into battle unarmed and unprotected—sometimes even barefoot—signs of how little value their lives had to those above them.

Princes, counts, and other nobles were the commanders of the army not because they possessed talent but simply because it was expected of them. They were often only remotely involved with their troops, leaving their homes to join them only when a battle was imminent, and then usually staying at a safe distance. Beneath them were junior officers hoping to gain future favors from the princes and counts by effectively managing their troops and winning battles for which the commanders could take credit.

Poor and Rich in Prerevolutionary Russia

The military attitudes were a reflection of nineteenth-century Russian society at large: The role of the poor was to perform services from which the rich would benefit, but the rich had little if any obligation in return. Contempt for what was seen as a fairly useless but extraordinarily privileged group at the top of Russian society grew throughout the nineteenth century, but it remained below the surface because there seemed to be little hope of changing things. The poor were mostly serfs, peasants who were legally bound to the land on specific estates, and thus were essentially the slaves of the estate holder. They lived in simple dirt-floored huts on a diet of thin soup and heavy bread. Some of the poor had fled serfdom to cities like St. Petersburg and Moscow, but once there they usually found more hunger and more mind-numbing work in factories.

The wealthy, on the other hand, traditionally had several homes—one in St. Petersburg, one in Moscow, and at least one country home, called a dacha. The royal family, the Romanovs, had numerous palaces, all filled with beautiful furniture and expensive decorations and artwork. Particularly in St. Petersburg, life for the rich was a nearly endless stream of parties, balls, and social visits. Though social unrest both in the cities and on the country estates generated occasional worry about maintaining their power and privileges, life was very pleasant for the Russian elite.

Peasants in nineteenth-century Russia lived a very meager existence and were completely obligated to the privileged classes.

RUSSIA INDUSTRIALIZES

By the late nineteenth century, however, several emperors of Russia, called czars, had noticed growing discontent among the poor and begun to realize that if they were going to stay in power they would have to be perceived as doing something for the people. In 1861 serfdom was abolished; peasants who had formerly been forced to stay on a particular piece of land could move to cities, hire themselves out as laborers on a noble's land, or become small, independent farmers. The number of schools for Russian children skyrocketed, as did the number and size of universities. Many, though still not all, poor children learned to read, and even could hope to attend the university if they were sponsored by an influential person such as a clergyman or noble. Little by little, the masses were gaining some control over their lives.

With literacy came new things to read, such as newspapers. Ordinary Russians, with education and information, thus began to form ideas about their place in Russian society. Because by now several million Russians were working in a few large cities and industrial towns, they had plenty of opportunity to share their new ideas with others. Political organizations critical of the Russian nobility formed. Discontent mounted as the twentieth century dawned, but because factory workers knew they depended on wealthy owners or the government for their livelihoods, discontent rarely surfaced.

Though the vast majority of people who flocked to the cities remained poor and were treated no better by factory owners than they had been by estate owners, a new middle class had also begun to emerge which included merchants and tradespeople such as butchers, cobblers, and seamstresses. They were self-employed, and thus were among the first to believe the country could do without the upper class altogether. Disinterested or unintelligent nobles might still get unearned credit for winning a battle, and their workers might bring in a good harvest without their guidance, but it took skill and intelligence to run a business, and the middle class felt that they deserved a more important role in government.

Groups formed in St. Petersburg and Moscow published papers and debated ideas about what a new and better Russia would be like. Particularly popular with many intellectuals in the late nineteenth and early twentieth century were the works of Karl Marx. His ideas included abolishing private property and creating a society with no upper class, in which people govern themselves and collectively own and share the profits of farms and factories. Though some found his ideas extreme, doing away with a society in which it was perceived that the nobles had all the power and the people did all the work was a popular idea.

THE GROWTH OF COLLECTIVES

Outside St. Petersburg and Moscow, life remained as hard as ever, and the distinction between rich and poor remained as clear as it always had been. Though the emancipation edict had freed the serfs, most found themselves unable to do much to improve their lives. According to historian John Channon, "Ploughing was still largely carried out by a wooden cultivator rather than by an iron or steel plough share. One-third of all peasant holdings was without a horse and another third had only one horse. Harvesting was by hand, using sickles and scythes, rather than by mechanical harvesters."[4] Though they were technically free, they remained dependent on the nobles to buy their crops because the peasants had no way to take their crops to distant markets. Nobles, practically speaking, still had all the power.

Communities survived by pulling together; actually, even before the serfs were emancipated, Russian peasants had formed village communes. The village rather than the individual had traditionally been responsible for turning over to the estate owner whatever percentage of the total harvest was demanded. As a result, peasant communes already had a well-established system of self-government based not on absolute equality but on a broader sense of fairness. For example, they might decide that an old woman who had lost her husband deserved supplemental grain, or that another family whose two grown sons returned every year from the city to help harvest crops should contribute a greater share of their grain to the estate owner than someone without similar help. Thus, though most peasants had never heard of Karl Marx, his philosophy of working together and pooling resources was already second nature to them.

THE FALL OF THE LAST CZAR

Thus, at the turn of the century there were two distinct kinds of poor, the urban poor and the rural poor, both looking for a

THE DEATH OF THE ROMANOVS

By the summer of 1918, Lenin was worried that the fledgling, un-popular Bolshevik government might be overthrown in a counterrevolution. To avoid giving supporters of the monarchy something to rally around, Lenin decided that it was time to get rid of the royal family, who were being kept captive in the dreary Siberian city of Ekaterinburg. There they lived in four poorly furnished rooms in what was euphemistically called the House of Special Purpose. By all accounts, a gentle and gracious family, they were victimized daily by vengeful, usually drunken guards, who spat in their food, whitewashed the windows so they could not look outside and watched them go to the bathroom. Some sources say they raped the czar's teenage daughters.

One night the family was told they were to be moved to another location. Dutifully they dressed and went to wait in a small basement room. Suddenly twelve soldiers crowded in the doorway and began shooting. Both the czar and his wife died quickly from shots to the head, but bullets apparently bounced off the chests of the daughters, who had sewn precious jewelry into their dresses. The soldiers then clubbed and bayoneted the moaning girls, their brother, and some servants for at least ten minutes. They were all carried from the house, some possibly still alive, and thrown down a mineshaft outside town. In a day or two their bodies were retrieved and buried in a shallow, unmarked grave, after their faces were smashed to make identification impossible. Later, when the grave was found, neither the czar's son or his daughter Anastasia's bodies were there, fueling already widespread speculation that one or both had managed to escape.

The viciousness of the murders, especially of the children, by what author Peter Kurth in *Tsar* calls a "drunken, sadistic band of thugs so . . . incompetent that they afterward needed three whole days to bury the bodies" continues to haunt the Russian people today. The profound disrespect shown for the Romanov family's lives and for their historical role is seen by many as the point at which communism ceased to be a morally just cause and became a power far worse and more brutal than Nicholas or his predecessors had ever been.

chance to better their lives. Along with the poor, a growing middle class increasingly resented the power of the rich, as did a small number of people who had received university educations and had skills and knowledge they intended to use to make drastic changes in their country. All of these developments—in the country and in the cities, among the poor and the better off—were enough to put rumors of revolution in the air.

From the mid–nineteenth century until the Russian Revolution of 1917, the czars, members of the Romanov family, tried to remain popular by walking a tightrope between granting reforms and greater freedoms and cracking down on dissent to prevent dissident movements from gaining strength. For instance, in 1881, Alexander II, considered a reformer for emancipating the serfs, was assassinated by a group called the People's Will, early advocates of communism. His son, Alexander III, responded by suppressing freedom of speech and assembly, and by blaming all of the problems of Russia on the Jews as a means to deflect attention from the real problem, the continued gap between the rich and the poor.

Alexander's son, Nicholas II, conceded the need for greater freedom than his father had allowed, but he was not really up to the task of ruling. According to historian John Channon, Nicholas "was very much a man out of time, ill-suited to his role as czar and with no desire to assume the mantle."[5] He became czar in 1894, inheriting a far more complex empire than that over which his predecessors ruled. Not only were the poor less willing to accept their fate, but many of the nobles were beginning to see that if they did not willingly agree to give up some of what they had, revolution might take it all. Nicholas was a weak czar at a time when a powerful public figure was needed to keep the respect of the Russian people. He was blamed for getting the

The Romanovs maintained power until the Russian Revolution in 1917.

country into an ill-advised war with Japan in 1904, and his German wife, Alexandra, was falsely rumored to be plotting a German takeover of some Russian territory.

Added to all these problems was the fact that the heir to the throne, Nicholas and Alexandra's only son, was a hemophiliac, subject to uncontrollable bleeding from even a scratch or a bump, and was unlikely to live to take the throne. Genuinely devoted to all their children, the royal couple, but particularly the empress Alexandra, fell under the influence of a charismatic monk named Rasputin, who claimed to be able to heal the young heir. Rasputin was by all accounts a hypnotic but disgusting man, and the fact that a man who, in the words of historian Rowlinson Carter, "carried with him a strong animal smell, like that of a goat"[6] had greater access to the royal couple than anyone else caused disrespect for the czar to grow.

Rasputin claimed that he had the power to heal the Romanov heir of hemophilia.

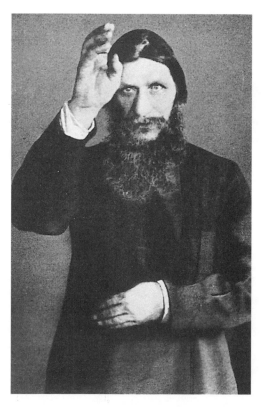

BLOODY SUNDAY AND THE 1905 REVOLT

In 1917 the Romanovs were overthrown and eventually executed, but the events leading to their downfall actually began in St. Petersburg twelve years before. In January 1905, on a day known as Bloody Sunday, a priest, Georgy Gapon, led a peaceful group of protesters to the Winter Palace of the czar to call attention to their poor living and working conditions. Army troops opened fire and mounted police trampled the crowd, killing several hundred people. Protests over Bloody Sunday spread nationwide. Peasants stormed nobles' homes and evicted them. "Soviets," from the Russian word for council, were set up in cities to organize strikes and protests, including one in St. Petersburg led by Leon Trotsky, who would become a leader of the 1917 revolution.

Nicholas was forced to make some concessions, including establishing the Duma, a house of representatives. However, the people were soon disillusioned by the Duma; it could not pass laws without the czar's approval, and if the czar was dissatisfied with the Duma he could simply dissolve it and

THE RUSSO-JAPANESE WAR

The vast Russian empire stretched at one point from the far side of the Baltic sea, in Finland, to the far side of the Pacific Ocean in Alaska. However, as Russia eyed its position at the end of the nineteenth century it was clear that other European nations were so strong that expanding Russian trading ability or territory on its western extremity was unlikely. Thus, Russia looked to its eastern borders and decided that it would focus on becoming a Pacific trading power instead. To begin expanding its Pacific trade, Russia made an arrangement with China to build railroads across two stretches of Chinese territory, which the Russians could then use to transport goods to and from the heart of Russia to the Russian port city of Vladivostok and the Chinese city of Port Arthur, where Russia had a naval base.

Japan worried that Russia's interest in expanding trade might mean an interest in expanding territory, and Japan wanted to keep the Russians out of the Korean peninsula. As a show of its intention to thwart this, the Japanese launched a massive surprise torpedo attack on the Russian fleet near Port Arthur. Russia was not in a good position to fight back because the railroads were not complete and it had no way to resupply and rebuild its naval force except by sailing all the way from St. Petersburg around Africa, across the Indian Ocean and up to the Sea of Japan. By the time the fleet arrived Port Arthur had fallen to the Japanese, and in a humiliating defeat, the newly arrived Russian navy, after months at sea, was demolished within hours by the Japanese navy. Czar Nicholas was forced to negotiate a peace in which Russia agreed to stay out of Korea, give up the base at Port Arthur, and turn over to Japan a small portion of Russia's northern coastal territory on and near Sakhalin Island. Nicholas had staked his personal prestige on expanding Russian power in the east, and when he failed, he came one step closer to his fall from power.

create a new one. Nicholas had been persuaded to accept the idea of the Duma only because he assumed it would be stacked with his supporters, but it did not work out that way. Nicholas dissolved four Dumas while he was still czar, but overall, the years of this first limited attempt at government by the people were a time of great progress for Russia. Health services were funded and fifty thousand new primary schools were opened as a result of acts of the Duma. In fact, many historians believe that if World War I had not broken out and changed the priorities and focus of the country, the Duma might have evolved into a truly representative organ of government. Had that happened, communism might never have taken root, and Russia might today be a constitutional monarchy like Great Britain, with both a royal family and an elected parliament that actually governs the country.

THE RUSSIAN REVOLUTION

But that was not to be. World War I brought devastation to Russia between 1914 and 1918. Millions of soldiers died, as did millions more civilians in areas occupied by the Germans along the Russian empire's western front. Use of the railroads to move troops and armaments meant that food could not get to cities, and people began to starve. Dissidents such as Vladimir Ulyanov, known to history as Lenin, a Marxist writer who had been living in exile in Switzerland, came back to fan people's hunger and discontent into a revolution.

The 1917 Russian Revolution actually took place in two stages, neither of which really involved the masses or even had great popular support. The first stage was the forced abdication of the czar and exile of the royal family. This was brought about early in 1917 by members of the aristocracy, not by an uprising of the people, as is commonly thought. After Nicholas's abdication, members of the Duma established a temporary government under the leadership of Aleksandr Kerensky. Their goal was to delay substantive political change until the end of World War I, after which open elections, a constitution, and widespread reforms were promised. But this was not acceptable to some workers and peasants, who had become convinced that a radical change to a Marxist state should happen immediately.

As the war dragged on it became apparent within a few months that the provisional government lacked the ability to end the war or keep order at home. Led by Lenin, the Bolsheviks, whose name means "majority," were the main opponents of the provisional government. Lenin knew that despite his party's name it lacked the support of even close to a majority of the people, because its call for immediate, sweeping changes frightened people. Thus, though Lenin pretended to support the idea of elections to replace the current Duma with people freely chosen by the people, he knew the Bolsheviks stood no chance of getting power that way.

Lenin never felt that a "people's government" meant a fairly elected one. He believed a group of citizens who had the best interests of their countrymen at heart—that is, himself and his supporters— should govern on behalf of the people. Thus, he wanted a country with only one political party—his own—and felt that elections should be held only within the leadership for positions of power, such as the presidency. He also believed that it would probably be necessary to establish and maintain this new order, at least at first, by repression and violence against the very people it was claiming to serve. Others would want to choose their country's path, but Lenin was sure once people had seen communism in action they would be glad the Bolsheviks had initially chosen that path for them.

The Russian Revolution began in 1917 before World War I ended in 1918.

Russia did hold open elections in mid-1917 after the czar's abdication. Lenin and his corevolutionary Leon Trotsky predicted correctly that the Bolsheviks would do poorly. Their supporters surrounded the building where the newly elected Duma was meeting, and forced it to disband. This, the second "phase" of the Russian Revolution, was so quick and so quiet that, according to historian John Channon, many people "went to work as usual without realizing what had happened."[7]

Thus the Russian Revolution ended, but establishment of a Communist state was complicated by the fact that the majority

RUSSIANS AND SERBS

In 1999 the government of Slobodan Milosevic began a campaign to rid the Yugoslavian province of Kosovo of its ethnic Albanian population. When the North American Treaty Organization (NATO) began a bombing campaign to force Milosevic to stop committing atrocities against the Albanians and forcing them to leave Kosovo, the Russian Federation was the most vocal opponent of the NATO effort. The Russians played a leading role in negotiations that brought the conflict to an end in June 1999, but startled the world when they suddenly moved in to occupy a part of Kosovo in advance of the arrival of NATO peacekeeping forces. Though President Boris Yeltsin claimed the occupation was unauthorized by his government, it was clear that Russians were concerned that if they did not move quickly Serbs, who had initiated the aggression against the Albanians in Kosovo, might end up with no place to live in Kosovo safe from retaliation.

Russia's concern for the Serbs is long-standing, and 1999 was not the first time that Russian alliances with the Serbs have made the region an international hot spot. In fact, World War I broke out over this same alliance. By 1914 the nation of Serbia was Russia's strongest ally in the Balkans, a region that includes Romania, Greece, Bulgaria, and Albania. When Austrian archduke Ferdinand was assassinated by a Serbian, the empire then called Austria-Hungary threatened to invade Serbia in retaliation and take away its independence. Russia went to Serbia's defense, and because of Germany's traditional alliance with German-speaking Austria, the Germans used Russia's announcement of support for Serbia as an excuse to declare war on Russia and another of Russia's allies, France. The result was World War I.

Russia's link to Serbia is a deep one. Both nations share the Eastern Orthodox faith and both nations are ethnically related, comprised mostly of Slavs. Russians clearly felt deeply about the loss of life and property of Serbs during the NATO air campaign, but in the 1990s no one wanted to repeat the mistakes of 1914. Thus, this latest struggle in the Balkans ended without escalating into a broader war.

of Russians had not actively supported the Bolsheviks. For several years, supporters of the monarchy, called Whites, fought the Bolsheviks, or Reds, in all parts of Russia. Eventually the Reds won, but, again, not because the average citizen supported them. As Lenin forecast, he resorted to violent suppression of those he considered enemies to the cause. The Cheka, or secret police, was established in 1918; its victims were killed, interned in concentration camps, or sent into exile in work camps in Siberia and elsewhere. A precedent had been set that would take millions more lives in the course of the century, as the Communists held power by whatever means necessary.

By the time Lenin died in 1924 he had accomplished little toward the goal of actually implementing a Communist state. Instead he had established a precedent of ruling without allowing challenge or dissent, and backing up power with violence and repression. Though now everyone called each other "comrade," and the leaders claimed to be committed to the good of the people, the present looked to most Russians every bit as repressive as the past. Power was still firmly in the hands of a small number of Communist leaders, and the people had as little control as ever over their lives.

A small number of Communist Party members, including Stalin (second row, second from left), Lenin (second row, third from left), and Trotsky (second row, fourth from left), claimed to represent the people.

2

THE SOVIET UNION: 1922–1991

Among the first steps in establishing communism was determining how much of the former czar's empire the Bolsheviks actually controlled, and what the new country should be called. The term "Russian" actually only applied to one ethnic group, the descendants of the medieval kingdom of Rus who lived primarily in the region around Moscow. Russia had never been an appropriate name for the czar's entire empire. After the 1917 revolution, for example, people of Ukraine would clearly be part of the new country because they were firmly in the hands of the Bolsheviks, but they were Ukrainian and not Russian at all.

Thus, in 1922, Russia, Ukraine, Belarus, and Transcaucasia (now Georgia, Azerbaijan, and Armenia) formed the Union of Soviet Socialist Republics (USSR), or in shorter form, the Soviet Union, to both recognize their ethnic distinctions and announce their solidarity as one nation. In the next two decades other countries would join the Soviet Union either voluntarily or by force; at its height the USSR encompassed roughly the same territory as the Russian empire under Nicholas II.

But though the boundaries of the USSR in 1922 were clear, it was considerably less certain what was really meant by a "soviet socialist republic." When Lenin died in 1924 he had shared his vision of a society of comrades working together for the common good, but had done little to make this vision a reality. That would be left to his successor, Joseph Stalin, and those who followed him. These leaders' differing views of the Communist state each shaped and in its own way contributed to the downfall of the Soviet Union.

STALINISM

Joseph Stalin ruled as a dictator from 1924 through 1953. With the slogan "Fifty Years' Progress in Five," he urged his countrymen to close the gap between the USSR and the industrial superpowers of the West. Following Lenin's plan, land and industries were socialized, or turned over to state ownership. Private property was outlawed and confiscated. People worked either in state-owned mines, farms, or factories or on huge collectives that were theoretically run by the workers but in fact were closely controlled by the state. Workplaces began building housing, schools, grocery stores, and other facilities such as hospitals for their employees. Under Lenin's and Stalin's plan, all of a worker's needs were to be met by the workplace, and in return the worker would labor hard and long to build a strong Soviet economy based on highly productive farms and industries.

During Stalin's reign of terror, millions of Russians were murdered for not completely embracing communism or his dictatorship.

Those reluctant to go along with collectivization and loss of private property soon learned the cost of being insufficiently "patriotic." Stalin's rule soon became a reign of terror. Stalin began a series of purges of those he thought did not support communism or his dictatorship, including Lenin's ally Leon Trotsky, murdered in exile in 1940 in Mexico City by a Stalin agent. Stalin's vicious and deliberate attacks on individuals were notorious, but it is his incomprehensible savagery toward the common people of his own country for which Stalin is now most remembered.

Stalin called anyone who seemed unenthusiastic about communism a "wrecker," a category in which he included even starving people who ate a mouthful of what they were picking in the fields and collectives that hoarded grain to get themselves through the winter. Wreckers were shot by the millions during Stalin's era or deported to work camps, where most of them died. Only recently has the full horror of Stalin's

THE KIROV MURDER

In 1934 the St. Petersburg Communist Party leader, Sergei Kirov, was murdered. Joseph Stalin, then the leader of the USSR, took the first train from Moscow to St. Petersburg, where he publicly slapped the police chief in the face as a way of showing his grief and outrage for the police department's failure to protect such a great man. Stalin was one of Kirov's pallbearers and even had the St. Petersburg ballet renamed the Kirov in his honor. Vowing to avenge the murder personally, Stalin himself, without assistants or witnesses, carried out the interrogation of suspects.

Stalin's apparent loyalty to an old friend was a sham, for it was Stalin himself who had ordered his murder. Earlier that year at a meeting of the Party Congress, a small group of Party members had approached Kirov to persuade him to stand for election as Party boss, in an effort to unseat Stalin. Kirov refused, but Stalin got wind of the plot and decided to eliminate even a reluctant potential rival. Despite the fact that the threat to him had been so mild, and that no more than a dozen individuals could possibly have been involved, by the next Party Congress was held five years later, 1,108 of the 1,966 delegates to the previous congress had been shot.

Typically, according to historian Brian Moynahan, prominent people such as these Party Congress delegates "were taken quietly and without fuss . . . off sidewalks, . . . between acts of *Swan Lake* at the Bolshoi, in the sleeping car of a train," often directly to an already dug grave in a nearby woods. No one was safe from what Moynahan reports one witness as calling "that frightful moment [when] they say to you 'your pit is ready.'"

Stalin ordered the murder of Sergei Kirov (right), the Communist Party leader, in an attempt to eliminate any party rivalry.

reign of terror been exposed. Evidence includes the discovery of mass graves, such as one near Minsk, where workers laying a gas pipeline in the 1990s uncovered a grave holding a hundred thousand bodies. Hundreds of thousands more skeletons have been found in abandoned mine shafts and quarries, or simply breaking through the earth's surface during spring thaws.

The mass murder of peasants was not only an atrocity but resulted in widespread starvation when there was no one left to harvest the crops. As many as 14 million peasants were victims of famine or murder during Stalin's regime; altogether as many as 20 million Soviet citizens died, but as his successor Nikita Khrushchev later admitted, "no one was keeping count."[8] The results of the 1937 census were suppressed because the peasant population had dipped so low. In keeping with the spirit of the times the members of the census board were shot as wreckers, for what Brian Moynahan quotes as "treasonably exerting themselves to diminish the population of the USSR."[9] Journalist Adam Hochschild points out that the census board murders illustrate that under Stalin, "execution was the favored solution to every problem, including those caused by previous executions."[10]

The mass murder of peasants left very few people to harvest the crops and resulted in widespread famine and starvation.

THE USSR UNDER KHRUSHCHEV

But the next Soviet leader, Nikita Khrushchev, wasted very little time distancing himself from his predecessor. At the 1956 Party Congress he delivered in closed session a "secret speech" that denounced Stalin and his actions in great detail. Khrushchev did have an idealistic streak, but he can hardly have been as shocked as he claimed to be about Stalin's activities, as he had in fact participated in some of them.

Khrushchev sincerely believed in the Communist vision of a society in which the people governed themselves in communities organized around highly productive farms and industries. His downfall was his overly optimistic view of how quickly and easily the Communist state could be achieved. Lenin had predicted that a period of repression was necessary before people would embrace his vision, but that period had now lasted over forty years and had claimed millions of victims. The average Soviet citizen was by this point quietly cynical about the Communist leadership and the Communist Party altogether.

Soviet leader Nikita Khrushchev denounced Stalin's actions while maintaining his belief in communism for Russia.

Khrushchev knew that his success would depend on making Soviet citizens enthusiastic participants in building the Communist state. His approach was to announce grand plans and programs which he promised would transform the

Soviet Union into a workers' paradise within only a few years. His excitement was not contagious. However, though he felt betrayed by people's general lack of enthusiasm, unlike Stalin and Lenin, Khrushchev was not a vengeful person. Though he was not above suppressing dissent with bloody force, as happened in 1956 in Hungary when the people attempted to overthrow their Communist government, the purges of Stalin's time did not recur under Khrushchev. In fact, Khrushchev's epitaph reads, "The fear's gone. That's my contribution."[11]

The epitaph is not entirely warranted, however. Though Khrushchev initially lifted censorship somewhat and released thousands of prisoners from the gulags, or prison camps, as a way of underlining his differences from Stalin, the secret police, renamed the KGB, continued to monitor and harass dissenters, and people were still encouraged to inform on each other. People considered enemies of the revolution still were removed from society by various means, but random and mass violence ceased to characterize Soviet life.

What did characterize Soviet life was indifference of the workers toward grand Communist goals. Khrushchev wanted to close the gap between Russian and American industrial productivity within only a few years, and to that end he put together (against the advice of his own economic experts) plans specifying to the last detail such things as the number of trucks or the ruble value of furniture each individual factory in the entire Soviet Union was to produce in a year.

The attempt to command the economy in such a detailed way proved disastrous. If an auto plant, for example, ran short on parts, rather than slow down production and not meet its commanded goal, it might turn out cars with three wheels. Quality control was so poor that tractors were commonly abandoned in fields for lack of a small defective part that could not be easily replaced because new parts were going into new defective tractors rolling off the assembly lines. Furniture factories whose goals were tied to the monetary value of the furniture they produced found it easier to make fewer pieces of more expensive furniture, such as huge sofas that would not fit in tiny Soviet apartments, or massive chandeliers that pulled down ceilings with their weight.

Khrushchev's optimistic goals proved similarly disastrous in agriculture. He was impressed by the cornfields and the cattle herds of the American Midwest, so he ordered huge stretches of southern and central Russia ploughed for corn, to be used to feed the huge cattle herds of his imagination. However, the Soviet Union is much farther north than the American Midwest, and the growing season is far too short for corn. Abandoned cornfields soon turned to dust bowls.

THE SPACE AND ARMS RACES

By the early 1960s Party leaders were secretly plotting to oust Khrushchev. He was both temporarily saved and eventually doomed by his attempts to match the United States as a military power. The Soviet Union produced its first atomic bomb in 1949, and the succeeding decades saw a huge arms buildup as each country sought to defend itself through policies of deterrence. Khrushchev, seeing a way to best the United States, also secretly put army scientists to work on a space program. In 1957 *Sputnik*, the first man-made satellite, was launched into orbit around the earth, and in 1961 the first astronaut, also a Russian, returned safely from space.

These signs of superiority lifted the spirits of the Soviet people and boosted the confidence of Khrushchev, who became known in the West for his claims that communism would soon "bury" the United States. In 1962, Cuban leader Fidel Castro encouraged Khrushchev to bring missiles to Cuba to aim at the United States. When President John Kennedy ordered a blockade of Cuba to intercept missile-carrying ships, Khrushchev was forced to back down, a retreat perceived as unforgivable humiliation by the Communist Party. When a few poor harvests and price increases on basic goods effectively erased the advances he could point to during his time in office, Khrushchev was quietly ousted from power in a 1964 coup.

Khrushchev's legacy, however, still affects the way Russians think today. They feared (and in a perverse way admired) Stalin, but they came to see Khrushchev as a bit of a fool, and the awe with which Russians traditionally viewed those in authority would never be completely restored. Additionally, Khrushchev encouraged Soviet citizens to see the United States and capitalism as great evils that threatened their very existence, and some of this leftover sense of peril has made it difficult for some Russians, particularly older

NIKITA KHRUSHCHEV

Nikita Khrushchev was born into a family of sheepherders in 1894. When he was fifteen his father moved the family to a coal-mining town because he thought life as a miner might be an improvement. Soon Nikita got a job as a pipefitter in a factory. According to historian Brian Moynahan in *The Russian Century,* "His progress in the Party had a classic ring to it: the borrowed copy of the *Communist Manifesto* at sixteen; the instant conversion to the cause; emergence as a strike leader in the plant; the sack in 1912 when the strike was broken." Being blacklisted for his political activities gained him some prestige among fellow Communists, and after the revolution he became chairman of the metalworkers' union, then a Party organizer for a number of mines.

Over the next few years Khrushchev rose quickly in the Party, which was anxious to overcome its intellectual image by promoting working-class people. He moved to Moscow to serve as supervisor of construction for the spectacular subway system of Moscow and eventually he became one of the few people close enough to Stalin to be regularly invited to dinner. Moynahan quotes Khrushchev as saying, "I was literally spellbound by Stalin. Everything that I saw and heard when I was with him bewitched me." When Stalin died, a battle of treachery and countertreachery for his job was waged between Khrushchev and Lavrenti Beria, head of the secret police. Khrushchev won by the time-honored Soviet method of arresting Beria on a string of charges, trying him quickly, and executing him immediately.

Though Khrushchev was hated by many for his rather abrupt and bullying personality and for his foolish schemes, he did engender some affection, because he was always perceived as a simple, energetic, and sincere man who had not forgotten his roots. Jokes about him abounded, but often reflected an appreciation for this very complex man who had come so far and believed so fervently in his cause. One such joke stated that probably the first people to fly to the moon would find a short, fat, beady-eyed man there telling them how to plant corn.

The Communist Manifesto *was the inspiration for Khrushchev's political career.*

LIFESTYLES OF THE PARTY CHIEFS

Communism calls for a "classless society," one in which people have no more and no less than they need. This ideal may have sufficed for most of their "comrades," but the Party elite, particularly under Leonid Brezhnev, expected far better than equal treatment. The new elite cruised through town in chauffeured limousines in a special VIP lane, and even had their own airports and special planes. Like the nobility of old, they feasted on caviar, fine brandy, and imported chocolates. Their children's futures were assured. They went to special schools and were ensured the best jobs upon graduation.

They were best known for their fancy vacation retreats on the Black Sea and other regions. According to historian Brian Moynahan, Brezhnev's mother once looked around at her son's huge vacation dacha and said nervously, "Well, it's good, Leonid . . . but what will happen if the [Communists] come back?"

ones, to accept the change to a more American-like market economy in Russia today.

THE BREZHNEV ERA

Nikita Khrushchev was perceived by Party leadership as a reckless man. His bossiness and unwillingness to take advice had offended nearly everyone around him. The Party was not about to make the same mistake again. The next leader was Leonid Brezhnev, under whom the Soviet Union entered into two decades of what historian Brian Moynahan calls "the big sleep."[12] The country's apparent prosperity was actually stagnation skewed by profits from huge Siberian oil reserves. Agricultural production was down, and Russians were increasingly being fed by imported food paid for with oil money. Industries continued pouring out shoddy goods, none of which were competitive in foreign markets.

Party leadership showed no outward signs of concern. By now the Party was ruled by old men who had lived most of their lives among the Party elite. They were as out of touch with the lives of average Soviet citizens as they were with Lenin's original vision. Though they continued to pay lip service to earlier ideals, they no longer saw their goal as a society without a privileged elite and in which a strong central government was unnecessary. Now Party leaders tacitly worked to perpetuate their own power and what were in many cases lavish lifestyles, and to keep the economic failure of communism from coming to light. They controlled discontent in part by allowing people to own things they had not had access to before, or in the words of Russian poet Yevgeny Yevtushenko, "buy[ing] us off like big children."[13] For example, between 1970 and 1975 the number of private cars doubled to 3.6 million, two thirds of Soviet homes got televisions, and half got refrigerators.

Outside the USSR, people's unhappiness with communism could not be contained so easily. The old tactics of force had to be used again in 1968 when nearly four hundred thousand Soviet soldiers invaded Czechoslovakia to quash a move toward democracy under Alexander Dubcek. When the Soviet army invaded Afghanistan in 1979 to prop up its shaky Communist government, the subsequent protracted war was seen inside the Soviet Union as a moral and political disaster. The Soviet Union lost over fifty thousand soldiers and its leaders lost any remaining respect they commanded among their own people.

During the Brezhnev era, party leaders were as out of touch with the average Soviet citizen as they were with Lenin's original communist vision.

MIKHAIL GORBACHEV

If Stalin's era had bred frightened respect and Khrushchev's had bred disrespect, Brezhnev's era bred cynicism among the Russian people. All of these feelings are still blended today in Russian attitudes toward their government. When Brezhnev died in 1982, and two successors, both old men, died within the next three years, the way was left open for a new generation of Soviet leaders.

Mikhail Gorbachev had been in the audience as a young man when Nikita Khrushchev gave his "secret speech" denouncing Stalin. Gorbachev thus became part of a new generation of Communists committed to the philosophy but opposed to past leaders' actions. In 1985 he was appointed head of the Soviet Communist Party; cautiously, he waited for powerful Party elite to die off, after which he began letting his views be known. Gorbachev had seen that the USSR could never compete globally without the free exchange of ideas and encouragement of creative thinking that had begun putting computers in American homes before the average Soviet citizen had access to a typewriter. Gorbachev saw that democratic institutions such as free speech needed to be part of any healthy government, whether communist or not, and that greater freedom would be the key to economic recovery.

In June 1988, Gorbachev proposed that the country's political leaders should be chosen by popular election rather than by the Communist Party elite. The only political party was still, of course, the Communist Party, and Gorbachev envisioned voters simply making choices among Communist candidates. When the first election was held in 1989, however, the Communist party was stung by the scope of its defeat. Gorbachev had underestimated the extent of existing resentment and disrespect toward the government. The most extreme example was in Lithuania, where non-Communist candidates running independently as representatives of various political interest groups won thirty-nine of the forty-two Lithuanian seats in the USSR's newly formed Congress of People's Deputies. Sensing that Gorbachev's reforms might represent a chance to free themselves of the Soviet Union, many of its fifteen republics began pressing for independence.

Gorbachev had indeed opened a Pandora's box with his two-pronged approach to change. The first prong was what he called "glasnost," or openness. This policy meant that the government would be more truthful with the people and that the people themselves would enjoy more rights, such as freedom of speech, religion, press, and assembly. The second prong of Gorbachev's approach to change was called "perestroika," which means restructuring, or reform of the economy. Long-simmering resentments came to a boil as economics and politics came out into the open for discussion, and Gorbachev quickly discovered that it was easier to announce new freedoms than to control what people did with them.

Even Russia, the republic at the core of the Soviet Union, which included half the Soviet population and three-quarters of its land, began taking advantage of the spirit of openness and reform. Under an energetic and fiery leader named Boris Yeltsin, formerly a protégé of Gorbachev, Russia began asserting its independence from Communist Party control. Yeltsin rose through the Russian parliament to become the president of the Russian Republic in 1991, becoming in the process Gorbachev's best-known critic. Yeltsin accused Gorbachev of focusing on flashier reforms such as freedom of the press and religion because he lacked the courage to tackle the rot at the core of the Soviet economy.

Unnerved by Russia's possible bid for independence, Gorbachev reimposed censorship and put more old-style Communists, or hard-liners, in positions of power. He lost nearly all his support by this move, because proreformers abandoned him and hard-liners already hated him because of his attempts at reforms. When Lithuania's bid for independence was put down at Gorbachev's direction by the army, his reputation for being different from his predecessors was tarnished beyond repair. Added to Gorbachev's woes was a major drop in oil prices, which put an end to the USSR's ability to stay afloat through oil profits. Soon store shelves were empty and Soviet citizens were blaming Gorbachev for everything.

FAILED COUP OF 1991

By this point, Gorbachev had come to the conclusion that Lenin and Stalin might have been right, that communism might only work on a large scale by repression and force. This

*Citizens of Moscow
enjoy a moment of
celebration after the
failed coup in 1991.*

disheartened him, and in 1991, he negotiated a treaty with
the fifteen republics, allowing immediate independence for
those who wished it and establishing greater democracy in
those that remained. Two days before the treaty was to be
signed, hard-line Communists attempted to overthrow Gorbachev and reassert strong Party control over the entire Soviet Union. Gorbachev was placed under house arrest in his
vacation dacha, while coup organizers ordered military
troops and tanks into Moscow.

    According to historian Ann Imse, "The plotters said later
they expected Gorbachev to cave in to their demands for a
crackdown. When he refused, they figured a couple of tank
divisions in the capital would be enough to scare everyone

into obeying."[14] But the people of the Soviet Union had changed. They had watched life seem to open up around them, and they did not want to go back. Even the KGB refused orders to take over the Russian parliament building and arrest Yeltsin. Police and soldiers refused to fire on protesters. The coup leaders surrendered and Gorbachev returned to Moscow, shaken by the fact that members of his own cabinet had been behind the coup attempt. Less than a week later, Gorbachev indeed cracked down, this time on the Communist Party itself. Its headquarters were shut down and its activities outlawed.

With the sudden fall from power of the Communist Party, the republics, led by Ukraine, declared independence. According to Ann Imse, "With the Party's power crushed, the dictatorial glue holding the Soviet Union together was dissolved. The Soviet empire had no reason to exist."[15] Within a few months it no longer did, when Boris Yeltsin and the rest of the republic presidents declared their countries independent. On December 25, 1991, Mikhail Gorbachev, president of a country that no longer existed, resigned. The workers' state envisioned by Lenin had died without ever really living.

3

RESTRUCTURING THE ECONOMY

As the Russian Federation struggles to find its way after communism, scarcely anything about its economy has not been shaken to the core. Because so much about a society hinges on the way people go about getting and spending money, when the economic structure of a country changes, very little else about life remains the same. A few decades ago Soviet people could joke that the farms and factories in which most of them worked "pretend to pay us, and we pretend to work,"[16] but as Russia tries to throw off the old command economy in favor of a market one, it is finding that both work and pay are no longer laughing matters.

THE LIFESTYLE OF THE SOVIET WORKER

In the past, the typical Soviet worker could joke about being paid because under communism almost everything workers needed, such as housing, schools, and medical care, was either free or inexpensive. Thus, Soviet workers had little need for substantial paychecks. In fact, the average Soviet worker paid only 5 percent of his income for rent. The government owned all the stores and set prices very low (even if it meant losing money), so even if there were occasional shortages of things like food and shoes, and limited choices when goods were available, there was never any problem affording what one could find. Though a family might have to wait years for a larger apartment or a telephone, affording goods or accommodations when they were available was not a problem. Life was hard, but Soviet citizens rarely saw themselves as poor because almost everyone lived the same way. Homelessness was rare, and if anyone went to bed hungry it was usually because of a shortage affecting everyone.

THE SOVIET WORKPLACE

Joking about pretending to work, however, shows a serious flaw in the Communist system. Soviet workers were guaranteed employment, but usually this meant long hours at dreary, repetitive jobs. Quitting was not usually an option because in many parts of the country only a few workplaces employed almost everyone. On the other hand, guaranteed employment meant it was nearly impossible to be fired, so people had little incentive to work hard or do their jobs well. The government goal of putting everyone to work meant that factories, farms, and government offices often had more employees than they really needed, and thus there was rarely a lot of work for each person to do. Thus, over the years, workers came to expect that they would spend much of a typical work day not working at all. For example, after government office workers arrived at work, women would often spend the first hour taking care of their hair and makeup, and men would immediately disappear on a long break.

Everyone was guaranteed a job under the Communist system of government.

Added to the problem of worker inefficiency was the fact that most factories and collectives were required to show their success by measures that actually ended up encouraging failure. In the United States, for example, a factory that could not

CHERNOBYL

In the middle of one night in April 1986, a deadly nuclear disaster occurred at the Chernobyl power plant in Ukraine, caused in part by the typical inattentiveness of many Soviet workers toward their jobs, and in part by the ease with which Soviet leaders lied. Engineers somehow lost control of a nuclear reaction in a poorly constructed reactor and huge amounts of radioactive material spewed into the air. The administrator at the scene did not tell the surrounding communities both because he felt panic was a more serious problem than radiation and because, according to Daniel Yergin and Thane Gustafson in *Russia 2010*, "disasters were never reported; the population was not to know that Soviet technology could fail."

Children played and swam the day of the explosion, absorbing radiation through soil, air, water, and food. Adults went on as usual with their day, having been told nothing. Several days later area residents were evacuated, but by then they all had been exposed to radiation equivalent to one thousand chest X rays. More than half a million workers dispatched to contain the reactor blaze and to try to seal the reactor in concrete labored for days and sometimes for months in the poisoned atmosphere. Thousands fell sick and died over the following months and years. Despite newly elected President Gorbachev's eventual candor about the accident after his initial denials, the official policy is still to downplay the incident. A decree was in force until 1991 that radiation was not to be listed as a cause of death on any death certificate in the Soviet Union.

David Remnick, author of the Pulitzer Prize–winning work *Lenin's Tomb: The Last Days of the Soviet Empire,* suggests that for many Russians the day of the explosion at Chernobyl marked the psychological end of the Soviet Union because it represented so clearly the indifference of the government toward its people. The Soviet Union symbolically began to melt down itself that April day.

The Chernobyl nuclear disaster was caused in part by the typical inattentiveness of the Soviet worker.

sell what it made would soon be out of business. In the Soviet Union, however, the central government set production goals for farms and factories that were often not tied to the eventual sale or use of its products. For example, farms were required to produce a certain number of tons of produce. It thus would not be in a farming collective's best interest to throw out rotting potatoes before shipping because this would reduce weight. If the rot spread to the whole shipment, this was not the grower's problem. An estimated 40 percent of Russian produce was lost during the Soviet era by careless handling between the fields and the store shelves.

Factories as well as farms had to meet production goals unconnected to the quality of their products. For example, shoe factories would be directed to produce a certain number of pairs of shoes each year. Under this system, neither the factory managers nor the workers had any particular reason to concern themselves with whether the shoes they made fit well or held together, or if they made the right quantities of each size.

Churning out unusable products resulted in a terrible waste of time, energy, and resources. Nevertheless, people needed food and clothing, and if potatoes rotted or shoes did not fit, the government ended up importing what Soviet workers failed to deliver. Inadequate Russian products frequently caused ripple effects. For example, if a machine part for an excavator was produced poorly, mining operations could be halted for months when machines containing the part broke down.

Quality of production was at times secondary to the problem that farms or factories were not producing what they claimed at all. For example, historian David Remnick, in *Lenin's Tomb: The Last Days of the Soviet Empire,* tells of a widespread scam among textile factory heads in Uzbekistan, now an independent republic but then part of the Soviet Union. "Brezhnev would call on the 'heroic peoples' of Uzbekistan to pick, say 20% more cotton than the previous year. The workers . . . could not possibly fulfill the order. (How could they when the previous year's statistics were already wildly inflated?) But the local Party leaders . . . assured Moscow that all had gone as planned. If not better!"[17] The government's production goals were fantasies, and local producers felt free to give the government a fantasy in return.

A system of bribery evolved from the level of local plant management and farms all the way up to the Party chiefs in Moscow. Local Party leaders who claimed they had met or

Farms were required to meet unrealistic levels of production, forcing Party leaders to be deceptive about the actual levels of goods produced.

exceeded production goals received large bonuses. They kept some bonus money for themselves and used the rest first to bribe the factory manager to keep falsifying records about plant production, and second to bribe higher officials not to ask questions or challenge the figures. Up and down the line people made money on the side by keeping their mouths shut about how little was actually being produced.

Their cynicism, however, is understandable. Party officials in Moscow announced a series of so-called five-year plans for all factories and farms in the entire Soviet Union. These plans simply announced what production would be. Party economists were ignored or fired if they expressed doubts about proposed goals, and knowledgeable people such as plant managers were not consulted. Saddled with unrealistic measures of success, and pressured by a network of people profiting from bribes, even ethical people found they had very little choice but to participate in the web of lies.

As long as factories kept belching smoke and food somehow appeared on the shelves of government stores, and as long as Party-controlled media trumpeted stories of huge harvests and industrial growth, everyone simply pretended that the five-year plans were actually successful. Thus, communism produced generations of managers and local Party officials who knew no honest way of doing business. It also produced millions of workers who were told that their halfhearted work, often in broken-down workplaces, had achieved economic miracles.

During Leonid Brezhnev's time in office, money pouring into the treasury from new Siberian oil fields enabled the Communist Party to hide the fact that the country's economy was in deep trouble. Later, when world oil prices fell, the illusion was shattered because suddenly reduced profits could no longer mask economic problems. If Russian wheat did not get to market, there simply was not enough bread. If raw materials did not get to factories, there were no belching smokestacks. By the time Brezhnev died in 1982 the economic disaster of Soviet communism was unmistakable.

COMMAND ECONOMY VERSUS MARKET ECONOMY

The heart of the problem in Soviet communism was what is known as a command economy. In this system businesses are simply told by the government what and how much they will produce, whether it be ball bearings, corn, or aprons. The government is responsible for deciding what the country needs and figuring out whom to order to do what. In contrast, a market economy is based on what economists call the law of supply and demand. In market economies such as the United States,' businesses are themselves responsible for figuring out what people will want or need to buy, and matching what the business makes or does to what they think will sell.

Market economies, therefore, reward innovation and creativity because people must continually introduce new products or improve old ones to maximize market share and profit. Market economies also reward hard work and good business practices. A factory owner in a market economy who lets broken machinery stay broken, or pays ten workers when one can do the job, or keeps making products that do not sell, or is indifferent to whether the product arrives in stores in salable condition, is soon out of business.

In contrast, the Soviet command economy stifled creativity and initiative by making little use of the minds of its workers to develop new or improved products or to think of ways to enhance production or work conditions. New technologies do not emerge when the only thing that is rewarded is cranking out more of what already exists, or when workers think it is someone else's job to have the all the ideas. The net effect today is that millions of Russian workers and even their bosses have not seen themselves as responsible for the work they do. They think work means simply doing what one is told—and as little of that as possible.

CREATING A MARKET ECONOMY

When Mikhail Gorbachev became president of the Soviet Union in 1985, he admitted openly that Soviet communism needed major reforms. He did not, however, want the Soviet Union to become like the United States. Gorbachev felt that money mattered too much to Americans and that making and spending it had made people greedy and unconcerned about the welfare of others and the good of the country. Gorbachev remained a committed Communist, believing that the economy could be revitalized without giving up the country's emphasis on the collective good rather than individual profit, as long as he and the Party had the power to keep reforms under control.

Still, Gorbachev knew his country lagged far behind Western Europe and the United States economically, and that the situation was getting worse because technology in the Soviet Union had stalled while the West leapt ahead. Soviet industries were still based around such things as huge steel mills, cement foundries, and strip mines, whereas the West had diversified beyond heavy industry into computers, space age plastics, and other new materials and technologies. While the Soviet Union was still trying to put telephones in homes, Americans had begun communicating in cyberspace.

Gorbachev took steps to reform the Soviet Union's ailing economy by privatizing state-owned businesses.

PRIVATIZATION

Among the first steps Gorbachev took to reform the economy was privatization, whereby state-owned businesses were turned over to groups of private citizens to own and run. Unlike in the United States, however, individuals could not start or run a business by themselves. Private businesses had to be cooperatives, the term used when a group of people finance and run a business and then share the profits. Gorbachev saw that people's motivation to work was tied to a belief that they would benefit from it, and he saw collectively owned businesses as a way of getting Soviet citizens excited about working harder while still maintaining the spirit of collective rather than individual labor and profit.

Gorbachev ran into problems with privatization almost immediately, stemming from the fact that, much as he might have

"GOD INSTRUCTS US TO SHARE"

According to David Remnick, in *Lenin's Tomb: The Last Days of the Soviet Empire*, in the Soviet Union of Leonid Brezhnev, "one of the most degrading facts of Soviet life [was] that it was impossible to be honest." Virtually all of even the most ordinary transactions in people's lives involved bribes, and people at the top, including Brezhnev himself, expected a cut of everything. The last two leaders, Gorbachev and Yeltsin, are perceived as considerably more honest, as reformers trying to gain control of organized crime rather than to profit from it themselves. So far they have fought a losing battle.

A mafia crackdown in progress.

An estimated three thousand to four thousand gangs, called mafias, operate across the Russian Federation. According to Daniel Yergin and Thane Gustafson in *Russia 2010*, they "sap the energies of [businessmen], rob them of profits that they might reinvest, terrify them, and paralyze . . . law enforcement officials." Yergin and Gustafson write that the mafia's typical greeting before they shake down or beat up a victim is "zaveshchaet delit'sia," which means "God instructs us to share." Unfortunately the share they take is one that hard-working business people have earned for themselves.

In a country without clear rules it is easy for the mafia to function without fear of the legal system. Their main fear is each other. Today in Moscow a business dispute is more likely to be settled with gunfire than negotiation. Recently an exclusive health club in Moscow had to advertise for new members because so many of its old ones were murdered in business deals gone sour or in retaliation for perceived invasions of someone else's racket.

There are thousands of privately owned businesses all over Russia.

wished it to be otherwise, the philosophy of communism and a market economy based on profit are incompatible morally and practically. To a Communist, if a person opens a hat store and uses the profits to buy a nicer house, that nicer house is proof that people's need for hats was exploited, because the owner obviously could have charged less for each hat. Today, with over a decade of experience with privatization, and the realization that the government will not support their daily needs, most Russians seem to have accepted that having money is necessary, and having a little more than someone else is not necessarily immoral. In Gorbachev's time, however, even modestly successful businesspeople were viewed as the moral equivalent of the scalper outside a sold-out rock concert.

The practical aspects of maintaining communism while giving people the freedom to make money for themselves were beyond Gorbachev's abilities. For example, he considered requiring that the majority of profits be turned over to the state, but he knew if that happened no one would see the point of opening a business. Gorbachev became increasingly uneasy with the effects of privatization, and his time in office was characterized by policy flip-flops that left everyone confused and contributed heavily to his downfall. Uncertainty about how privatization would end up working made few people willing to take the risk of starting a business. Today, no longer under the mantle of communism many of these early problems have been resolved, and there are many thousands of private businesses all over Russia, from kiosks selling cigarettes, to small stores in shopping malls, to collectively owned steel mills.

THE BUSINESS ENVIRONMENT TODAY

Getting privatization off the ground in the 1980s turned out to be the easy part. Today, caught halfway between a market and a command economy, Russian businesses struggle to survive. Sometimes getting necessary materials is difficult because there is no longer a central authority commanding that these materials be produced and delivered. For example, a soap manufacturer must rely on other companies to supply raw materials, utility companies to provide electricity and water, and perhaps a trucking company to transport the finished product from the plant to market. Businesses in Russia today cannot assume a reliable chain of production of goods and services exists.

But the problems of businesses go far deeper. The government also can no longer command that businesses follow certain rules, and the court system is so inefficient that businesses that cheat are likely to get away with it. Likewise, the growth of the Russian mafia has demoralized the business community because they lose much of their profits to protection rackets and other shakedowns.

Some businesses are also burdened by government control. The gigantic industry Uralmash, which builds heavy machinery for mining, illustrates the problem. The Uralmash general director dreams of someday "gaining the freedom to pick his own products, set his own prices, [and] choose his own customers,"[18] all things Western businesspeople take for granted. However, government contracts for outdated and unneeded huge mining excavators have kept the corporation from having the time and resources to retool its production line to turn out the smaller, more versatile machines for which Uralmash's general director has a long list of back orders. To make matters worse, the heavy equipment Uralmash is forced to make

BUILDING A BUSINESS BRICK BY BRICK

Mark Masarsky is an example of the flexibility and creativity—and some might say the flaunting of the law—needed to establish a successful private enterprise in Gorbachev's Soviet Union and in Putin's Russia today.

Masarsky's business is bricks. In 1978, as a political favor, he was given a chance (and a government loan) to buy a former prison including a factory where the inmates had worked making bricks. His arrangement with the government was to give it the first 12 million bricks he made each year and the rest would be his to sell. Using the prison cells as a dormitory, he soon had ninety resident brick makers and was making well in excess of the required number of bricks.

If Masarsky had decided to sell the bricks for profit, he would have been heavily taxed. Instead, he sold the bricks at the going state rate, but used their scarcity as a form of barter. Hedrick Smith, author of *The New Russians,* quotes Marsasky as saying that "bricks are better than money. . . . I sell four million bricks to the Volsky automobile factory for the fixed state price, and I make it part of the deal that they must sell me trucks, earth movers, and other equipment I cannot get from the state. I pay them [for the equipment] of course, but that is how I get the machinery I need." Likewise, he ensures a supply of gas and electricity to the plant by linking sale of bricks to a promise of consistent supply.

His deals have enabled him to grow to over 750 workers and to diversify into building houses. Smith quotes Masarsky's chief engineer: "We began two years ago with no moving equipment. . . . Now we have one hundred twenty pieces— trucks, bulldozers, cranes, excavators. When I look at all that I am amazed. Two years ago the most private property you could own was a motorbike or a car. Now we have all this."

is unprofitable because Uralmash must accept state-set payment that hardly covers costs. Thus, Uralmash, unable to build a profitable export business, barely breaks even and does not have the money to upgrade its dilapidated facilities.

THE NEW POOR

The transition from command economy to market economy has hurt Russians in their daily lives as well. For every person who has figured out how to make a profit under the new system there are hundreds whose circumstances have worsened. According to Donald N. Jensen, associate director of broadcasting of the prestigious European news service Radio Free Europe/Radio Liberty, "The post-Soviet transition has . . . generated a large number of 'losers.'"[19]

Approximately 1 to 2 million Russians are doing substantially better under privatization and another 5 to 10 million are doing somewhat better. Eighty million are suffering, however, as measured by the fact that they have to spend more than half what they earn just feeding themselves—quite poorly at that. Homelessness is an increasing problem, especially in the larger cities. Life expectancy has actually decreased, in part because living conditions for many are brutal. Sadly, protest by those who feel they are losing ground in the market economy, according to Jensen, "often takes individual, non-political forms such as the refusal to pay taxes, alcoholism, and suicide."[20]

A GOVERNMENT WITHOUT MONEY

Refusal to pay taxes is widespread, in part because taxation is an unfamiliar idea. In the Soviet era taxes were not necessary because nearly all goods were already turned over to the government. Currently, efforts to establish a taxation system

Homelessness is an increasing problem in Russia, especially in larger cities.

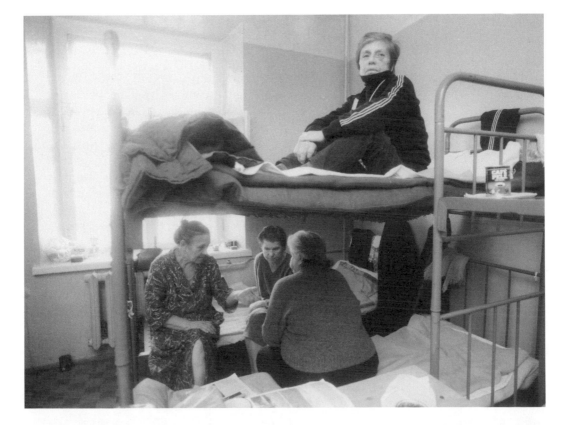

with clear rules and means for enforcement is one of the top priorities of the Russian government, but getting individuals to pay has been difficult. Getting businesses to pay is equally hard because their profits are usually small to begin with and have been made smaller by mafia shakedowns. Without revenue, the government cannot fund such social programs as education and health care, and public works such as roads and railroads go unrepaired.

 ## A FRIGHTENING LEGACY

Because of the nuclear disaster at Chernobyl, Russians are more acutely aware than many developing nations of the need to protect both the environment and people from the damage that can come from casual attitudes. Environmental groups are very active and have had some successes. However, most people are considerably less aware of another leftover problem from the Soviet era. Since Russia hit hard economic times at the end of the cold war, the military budget has been cut as much as 70 percent, and Russia can no longer afford to maintain high-tech facilities such as Krasnoiarsk-26, which makes plutonium for nuclear weapons.

Though two of the three nuclear reactors at Krasnoiarsk-26 have been shut down, the third continues to operate because it also supplies electricity for the one hundred thousand residents of the surrounding community. The problem is aggravated by the fact that the plant stores large quantities of radioactive waste as well as plutonium. According to Daniel Yergin and Thane Gustafson, authors of *Russia 2010*, cutbacks in weapons orders mean that "workers have nowhere to go. Work standards are dropping, workers are showing up drunk, and managers warn that an accident at their plant could be equal to 'several Chernobyls.'"

Though few would like to see a return to the cold war, when the Soviet Union was a major military power, in that era it allocated money for state-of-the-art nuclear facilities and had absolute control over access to dangerous weapons. Now, not only plants like Krasnoiarsk-26 are threatened, but so are many weapons storage facilities that lie, since the breakup of the Soviet Union, in areas outside the Russian Federation. This poses the risk not just of nuclear accidents but deliberate theft of weapons of mass destruction.

THE COLLAPSE OF THE RUBLE

The chaotic transition to a market economy led to another crisis, the collapse of Russia's currency, the ruble, in 1998. The ruble worked perfectly well within Russia, just as play money works perfectly well in a board game. The crisis occurred because Russia uses rubles to buy and sell products abroad. Because no one could figure out what a ruble was worth, no one knew what to charge for purchases in rubles. Practically speaking, the ruble became worthless abroad because no foreign trade partner would accept it. It will take time for the country's currency to stabilize at a value other countries will recognize, so international business can be resumed. The uncertain value of the ruble has caused soaring inflation, or price hikes, as businesses, fearing that the ruble will fall further, scramble to make sure they have charged enough to cover their costs. The result, of course, is that even fewer Russians have enough money to cover basic needs.

According to the Economist Intelligence Unit, a leading online analyst of the international economy, the collapse of the ruble "has ushered in a period of extreme political and economic uncertainty."[21] Russian citizens are used to having their income dovetail with their expenses. Those days are gone. Now, the average Russian who wants, for example, a pair of Austrian shoes, probably cannot afford to buy them. Increasingly there seems to be little the average Russian can afford. Their wages are still very low—too low in comparison with the price of basic necessities. Russians today are angry about what seems to be yet another in a long string of hardships they have endured at the hands of their government. Many now look back and think that things were better under the Communists, when the government assured their needs would be met, even if the price of that assurance was their personal freedom.

Russia has faced problems in the last two decades as big as the changes it is trying to make, and the collapse of the ruble was actually seen by economists as a necessary step toward a realistic economy. It is still too soon to tell whether Russia will be successful at charting a new economic course that answers the desires of its people for stability, sufficient money to meet their needs, and greater personal opportunity. One thing is clear, however: for the present, Russians must continue to live without guarantees.

4

POLITICS AND
NATIONHOOD

In the Soviet Union, the state commanded much more than the economy. The single, all-powerful political party simply announced who the leader of the country was and what the laws were. The Communist Party controlled the political life of the nation, from what children would be taught in school in Kiev, to what would be reported in newspapers in Murmansk, as well as what would be grown on a farm in Odessa, or how much toilet paper would be shipped to St. Petersburg. Thus, when the Soviet Union collapsed, more than the command economy collapsed with it.

Nowhere has the confusion of today's Russia been more noticeable than in politics. Just as the conflict between command and market economies is based on the question of whether the individual or the government should control business, the chaos in the Russian government stems from a similar question about who should have what powers. This question has two distinct parts; first, whether the president should have more power than the legislature, and second, whether the central government should have more power than regional authorities.

Many feel Russia should be led by a very strong person with a great deal of power because that leader could then take decisive, quick steps to end confusion and establish order. A leader who commands has been the tradition for centuries, and supporters of this view believe that the problems of the twentieth century have been caused not by rulers having too much power but by their abuse of it. If leaders could somehow be kept from exploiting their power and be made to respond to people's problems and concerns, many feel a kind of dictatorship would be the best direction for Russia in these chaotic times. Others feel that short-term chaos is a necessary price to pay in moving toward a democratic government in which the president has limited power and both regional governments and the national legislature have the main role in makings laws and setting policies.

SHOCK THERAPY

The widely reported disagreements between the Duma and President Boris Yeltsin hinged in part on the relative power of the presidency and the legislature, and in part on the specific goals Yeltsin tried to achieve. Yeltsin rose to power by criticizing Gorbachev's slow and seesawing approach to economic reform. Yeltsin advocated the quickest possible removal of government control over private enterprise. This approach has

BORIS YELTSIN

Boris Yeltsin's ability to win tough fights and survive disasters seems to have been with him since birth. At his baptism a drunken priest forgot he had left Yeltsin in the ceremonial font, and his mother saved him from drowning. His crooked nose was caused by a blow from a cart axle in a teenage brawl, and the missing two fingers of his left hand resulted from his youthful attempt to see how a hand grenade was constructed.

But the rough world of politics did not interest the young Boris. Unlike many previous Russian leaders, Yeltsin entered politics rather late, joining the Communist Party in 1961 at age thirty largely as a way of promoting his engineering career. He quickly came to Mikhail Gorbachev's attention as exactly the kind of daring, energetic young reformer the new Soviet leader was looking for. Yeltsin was put in charge of the Communist Party organization in Moscow, but he soon became critical of what he felt was the overly slow pace of reforms under Gorbachev. Yeltsin's public criticisms soon got him expelled from the Communist Party. Undeterred, Yeltsin turned to politics in the Russian Republic rather than in the central Soviet government. He became a member of parliament and then ran for president of the Russian Republic and won.

Thus, by the late 1980s Yeltsin and Gorbachev were forced into a rivalry of near equals, because what was Russia and what was the Soviet Union was sometimes difficult to tell apart. Moscow, for instance, was both a Russian city and a Soviet city, so the question of who was in charge in Moscow (and the rest of Russia) was not clear. Yeltsin stepped up his criticism of Gorbachev's seesawing reforms, and eventually was able to bring about Russia's independence and Gorbachev's fall.

Despite Yeltsin's ill health—he suffers from both heart disease and chronic alcoholism—he held off political challenges throughout his presidency, and in a move that surprised many, he suddenly resigned in late 1999, naming Vladimir Putin his successor. Though no longer President, his links to Putin ensure that Yeltsin will continue to influence Russian politics in the future.

been labeled shock therapy—the equivalent of jumping into cold water rather than wading in slowly. Yeltsin felt that a quick and comprehensive move to a market economy would actually be more effective in less time than taking slower steps.

One example of Yeltsin's shock therapy was lifting price controls in 1992. Farming collectives were hoarding their harvests gambling that prices would go up. City dwellers who relied on those collectives for food were going hungry. To resolve this, Yeltsin immediately removed price controls and the collectives let go of the food at much higher prices. That was good in the short run for those farmers, but bad for the people in the cities, who did not have the money to pay the resultant higher prices for bread and other food. According to historian Ann Imse, "Suddenly, most Russians realized they were poor. Almost overnight everyone and everything, from workers to factories, needed 10 times as much cash to operate and the money did not exist."[22] Such crises have led many to believe Yeltsin moved too fast and without a clear enough overall plan to transform the economy. The result, they feel, has been the hardships Russians now face in their daily lives.

YELTSIN VERSUS THE DUMA

Yeltsin was president of Russia from 1991 to late 1999, when in a surprise move he resigned and appointed Prime Minister Vladimir Putin to the position. Yeltsin's strong personality was matched by those of his opponents, and this factor, combined with genuine philosophical differences both about the president's powers and Yeltsin's specific programs, resulted in a government standoff that worsened the problems of the Russian people, who were simply trying to survive and figure out what the new rules are. Yeltsin lost more support than he gained over the years for his policy of pushing ahead with economic reforms regardless of the short-term consequences. He reasoned that if more money reaches Russians' pockets they will be able to afford higher prices. This could only be done, he believed, by speeding up privatization, so people could start making profits and wages could rise.

Russia was being pushed headlong into a market economy throughout the 1990s. The results frightened people. No one could say for certain what would happen next. People were being told to take care of themselves when they had no way to do so. Money was the key, and they had none. Suddenly the security of the old way of life was the only thing people could remember, and support grew for both Communist politicians and anyone else who seemed to promise an end to the chaos and misery.

Within the Duma, hard-line Communists saw this widespread discontent as a sign that they might be able to unseat Yeltsin, and even some of his former supporters began quietly plotting against him. According to Ann Imse, "By 1993 it was clear that the Russian political landscape was divided by a huge faultline, with president on one side and parliament on the other."[23] In 1993, Yeltsin exercised what he claimed was his right to dissolve parliament, but the Duma members rejected that claim and refused to leave office. Some barricaded themselves inside the parliament building. Over the next few weeks the crisis escalated as Yeltsin tried to starve out the Duma members and riots broke out in the streets.

Widespread discontentment with Yeltsin spread within the Russian legislature, known as the Duma.

Eventually, after civil unrest resulted in full-scale gun battles in the streets of Moscow, Yeltsin ordered the army to end the standoff by shelling the parliament building and setting it on fire. The Duma members behind the plot resigned, and Yeltsin called for national elections, both to replace the Duma and to vote on a hastily written constitution that gave broad, strong powers to the president.

THE 1993 ELECTION

The election of 1993 was bitterly contested, and both Yeltsin and his proposal for the constitution barely won. In the Russian Federation, unlike in the United States, candidates run for office independently rather than as party nominees. Thus, though Yeltsin won, the party most closely associated with Yeltsin's political ideas, Russia's Choice, actually got only 16 percent of the vote. The revived Communist Party received 12 percent. Surprisingly, however, the top vote getter, with 23 percent, the Liberal Democrats, whose hero was presidential candidate

Vladimir Zhirinovsky, whose grab bag of ideas included Russian ethnic superiority over other groups, anti-Semitism, and military confrontation with the United States and its allies.

Yeltsin, thus, was victorious in some respects but not in others. He was president, with a constitution giving him power to make changes. However, he had inherited a nightmare—a Duma with two opposition parties who could agree on little else except a desire to undercut him, and whose combined vote could succeed in doing so. It is a nightmare which his successor has inherited from him.

THE RUSSIAN CONSTITUTION

Vladimir Zhirinovsky (left) expresses his extreme political ideas, including Russian ethnic superiority over other groups, to a crowd in southern Russia.

Having a constitution, however, was a major step forward. Previous Russian constitutions had been little more than pieces of paper. The provisions in this constitution were a matter of law and could not be taken away except by a two-thirds vote of the legislature. Declaring that "the individual and his rights and freedoms are the supreme value,"[24] the

constitution guaranteed a free press, free speech, the right to own property, and the opportunity to travel freely. It also established social rights such as free education and medical care, and unemployment protections.

The constitution also provided a framework for resolving conflicts between the president and the Duma. The president was now clearly the highest official, the head of state. A group of government ministers, headed by a prime minister, was responsible for the day-to-day business of government. The elected legislature, the Federal Assembly, was divided into two houses, the most important of which was the Duma. The other house, the Federative Council, was made up largely of governors and leaders of the republics within the Russian Federation, and had only limited powers. The prime minister was to be nominated by the president and approved by the Federal Assembly. The president had broad powers to dissolve an uncooperative Duma, appoint and dismiss all other ministers, and in some cases issue orders without the approval of the assembly.

HANGING ON TO POWER

The 1993 elections thus established the powers of the president and the Federal Assembly. Still, dissent and resistance to Yeltsin's ideas, and ego clashes between Yeltsin and other presidential hopefuls, kept Russia adrift throughout Yeltsin's presidency. Yeltsin was seen by some as a hero for facing down the Duma before the 1993 elections, and as a man of great courage for not backing down in any crisis, but others saw him as a terrible example of the power-hungry kind of leader Russia was supposed to have moved beyond. Yeltsin never regained the popularity he had when campaigning against Gorbachev or when facing down the Duma to end the coup against Gorbachev. Unlike his predecessor, however, he managed to hold on to his job and name a successor whom many feel he can manipulate.

When presidential elections were held again in 1996, polls showed Yeltsin was likely to lose to the Communist candidate Gennady Zyuganov. Yeltsin secretly hired American political consultants to orchestrate a media campaign to undermine Zyuganov. Yeltsin won, even though he no longer had much real popularity, because he was able to scare Russians away from a Communist candidate by a media barrage of reminders of Soviet repression and terror. Yeltsin himself rarely campaigned, due both to heart problems and to his campaign managers' concerns about incidents of public drunkenness that had harmed his credibility as a leader.

After the 1996 election, Russian politics, like much else in Russia, remained in disarray. Yeltsin did not have sufficient support in the assembly to confirm his preferences for prime minister, and had to settle for compromise candidates who then did not work on his behalf to gain the support of the assembly for his reforms. In 1998 alone there were three changes of prime minister, and in the first half of 1999 there were three more.

Donald N. Jensen, associate director of broadcasting of Radio Free Europe/Radio Liberty, speaking of Russia's former president prior to his departure says, "Yeltsin has not exercised power so much as try to hold on to it from all chal-

A man shows his support for Gennady Zyuganov, the Communist Party leader.

Boris Yeltsin (left) appointed Vladimir Putin, a little-known politician, as prime minister of the Russian Federation in 1999.

lengers . . . to prevent any rival from emerging."[25] According to Jensen, Yeltsin was not above blackmail and bribery to keep opponents at bay, using "material incentives—money, apartments, and limousines—to coopt officials over whom he does not have . . . power."[26] Squabbles among Duma members also helped. According to Jensen, "Although opposition factions have dominated the Duma and have frequently denounced the president's policies, they have disagreed among themselves over strategy and tactics and often appeared more interested in maintaining their privileges than standing up to the president."[27]

A major reason Yeltsin retained power was that there was no widespread agreement on a better alternative. Yeltsin took care of this problem by stacking the deck in favor of his hand-picked successor, Vladimir Putin, who was a little-known politician when he was named prime minister and then president in 1999. Putin was able to run as an incumbent, a huge advantage no other candidate was able to overcome. Since his election, Putin has used renewed fighting in Chechnya as a way of diverting attention from the nation's other problems, but he has not been able to build any widespread support among the people. Likewise, he has had no more luck than Yeltsin in controlling the Duma.

Putin suffered a great political embarrassment in late 2000, when a Russian submarine sank and he refused to ask other nations for help rescuing trapped crew members until it was too late to save them. Many in Russia and the rest of the world remember how past leaders would never admit when there was a problem, and when a letter found on the submarine revealed that many crewmen lived for days and could have been rescued, Putin looked just like another in a long line of discredited and unpopular leaders who stood by while fellow Russians suffered.

RUSSIFICATION

Conflict between the president and the Duma is only one of two major political battles in the Russian Federation today. The other is between Russia and the other republics in the federation. The issue revolves around the relative power of Russia and ethnic Russians in relation to other regions and groups. The history of such conflicts is complex, and emotions run high about what is called "Russification."

Russification refers to efforts, over the centuries but especially during the Soviet era, to establish a common culture across vast stretches of land and among hundreds of ethnic groups. Because ethnic Russians were most numerous, Russian lands the largest, and Russians dominant in politics and culture, Soviet leadership took for granted that the unifying culture would be Russian. During the period after the 1917 revolution, when the Bolsheviks were consolidating their hold over the former czar's empire, Lenin wanted not to appear as if Russians had simply invaded and conquered Ukraine, Belarus, and other regions, but as if many different groups convinced of the superiority of communism had come together voluntarily. Because this was not the case, a rather inconsistent policy evolved of respecting the different ethnic regions while at the same time trying to create one Soviet culture, which meant in effect making non-Russians act more like Russians.

Russification had several different elements. Schools were required to teach in Russian regardless of the dominant language of the area. Likewise, a person could not attend a university or have a career in the military unless he or she spoke Russian and did not come across as odd or foreign. Russification also took the form of encouraging Russians to move to areas where other ethnic groups were dominant. For example, the Soviet Union centered its space program facilities in Kazakhstan, a large southern region now an independent country. They claimed this showed their support for non-Russian regions, but the net effect was that many Russians moved there to be part of the space program, and thus the Russian culture in the region was strengthened.

Russification under the Soviets also worked in reverse. Promising young non-Russians, such as Ukrainian Nikita Khrushchev, were brought into the Soviet elite in Moscow to rid them of too much regional influence and make them better Soviet rather than ethnic citizens. Migration by non-Russian farmers and industrial workers into Russian areas was encouraged as well.

THE GROWTH OF ETHNIC CONFLICT

The very existence of these ethnic regions was to play a key role in the eventual downfall of the Soviet Union. Despite the pretense of valuing ethnic groups, from Lenin on the real Soviet goal was to downplay people's pride and identification with any ethnicity, including Russian, in favor of identifying only as Soviet citizens. Ethnic Russians saw themselves as superior intellectually and culturally, but even their religion, national holidays, and folk arts were discouraged.

Russification was primarily a practical matter, stemming from a need for a common language with which to conduct the business and politics of the nation. Still, non-Russians saw Russians as oppressive killers of their cultures. Russians in turn felt that their culture had been destroyed because, had there not been a separate Soviet identity to create, the Russian culture might have been left alone. A helpful analogy is the issue of singing Christmas songs in American schools. In an attempt to treat cultures equally and show tolerance of diversity, Christmas carols have given way in many places to nonreligious holiday songs. This has left at least some Christians (and others) feeling that something important and beautiful has been lost. Russians

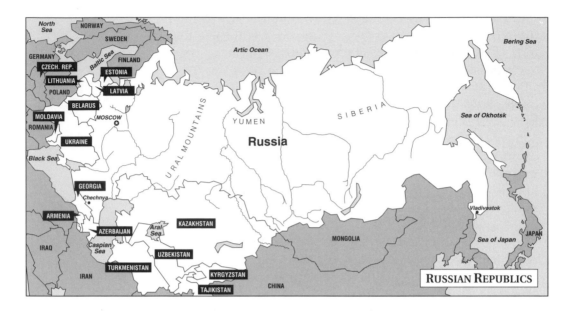

found themselves in a similar situation, and their resentment built against those they held accountable for their cultural losses. On the other hand they were resented in turn by non-Russians, who found Russian claims of cultural loss petty in comparison with their own.

THE BREAKAWAY REPUBLICS

Ethnic resentment against Russians and the Soviet Union exploded when Gorbachev took power and free speech was allowed. Ironically, the establishment of ethnic homelands by Lenin as a means to build the Soviet Union became the cause of its downfall. Countries such as Latvia took their status as ethnic republics to mean they had a choice about being in the Soviet Union. When Gorbachev made it clear that he was not prepared to hold the Soviet Union together by force, one by one the Soviet republics rimming the western and southern borders of Russia began asserting their independence.

Gorbachev's plan was to form a new union that would keep Communist countries together but make them more equal. He did not anticipate the depth of negative feeling toward the Soviet Union in the outlying republics, or the possibility that Russia, the giant republic in the Soviet Union, would itself declare independence, as it did in 1991. Without Russia there could be no Soviet Union. Gorbachev found himself outmaneuvered by Boris Yeltsin, who as president of Russia now had a country to lead, whereas Gorbachev had none. In 1991, the Union of Soviet Socialist Republics passed into history and the Russian Federation was born.

THE RUSSIAN FEDERATION

The Russian Federation today comprised of 21 republics; 49 regions, called oblasts; 6 territories, called krais; and 10 districts, called okrugs. The republics, few of which have any name recognition outside Russia, such as Tatarstan and Baskortostan, are each the traditional homeland of a non-Russian ethnic group such as the Tatars and the Bashkirs. Confusion about territorial boundaries has come about because some of these units overlap and because some have simply announced their existence without ever being formally recognized. Thus, the administrative divisions are an accurate reflection of the confusion in the Russian Federation today. What is clear, however, is that none of the regions in the Russian Federation will be able to leave without a fight the way the former Soviet republics did. Though most recognize they could not survive economically on their own anyway, a few regions have made their desire for independence known, and this has created a great deal of conflict in the federation today.

CHECHNYA

Chechnya, a small southern republic between the Black and Caspian Seas, had particular reason to want to rid itself of Russia. The Chechens were one of the ethnic groups singled out for annihilation by Stalin; in subsequent eras they endured decades of Russification by the same culture they held responsible for their near destruction. When Chechnya declared its independence in 1992, Russia was far too occupied with other political problems to do anything about it. It left the declaration unacknowledged, then several years later decided to fight the move to secede. Boris Yeltsin would later call the subsequent 1995 military invasion his greatest mistake in office. Many, including journalist David Remnick, have called it "Yeltsin's Vietnam."[28]

When one of Yeltsin's generals claimed that he could put down the independence bid in a two-hour military operation, Yeltsin put aside his image as a new and different, more democratic leader and gave his approval. The Chechens, however, had been preparing for Russia's eventual move for several years and mounted strong guerrilla resistance to the Russian army.

Yeltsin and his generals were drawn progressively deeper into the war because they could not stand the embarrassment of their inability to win. Ultimately, thirty thousand people, military and civilian, were killed, and the country was devastated. The war ended in a stalemate, with Russia agreeing to consider independence in a few years, and Chechnya largely ignoring the Russian government.

In 1999, hostilities between the Russian government and Chechnya were renewed. Claiming that a series of bombings in Moscow and St. Petersburg were the work of Chechen rebels, Putin claimed that the only way to put an end to terrorist attacks was to destroy the resistance movement in Chechnya altogether. Though many civilians have been killed or wounded by Russian attacks on Chechen cities and towns, once again the Russian government has been unable to break the strong resistance of the Chechens.

After centuries of unsuccessful foreign attempts to invade Russia, the Russian people have a saying: Only the Russians can conquer Russia. As political chaos continues, some wonder whether Chechnya may only be the beginning of the end of what may be a very brief Russian experiment with a more democratic form of government. In a nation without clear rules and without a past history of coming together to solve problems, it may come to pass that only the Russians can destroy their country as well.

5 CHANGES IN DAILY LIFE

The daily lives of Russians since the fall of communism have changed dramatically. In every aspect of life, the growing power of money and the waning power of the government to control and meet the needs of society are at the heart of these changes. Basic needs for food and shelter are no longer met by the government as they were under communism, and thus Russians are trying to provide for themselves things they once took for granted and without which they cannot survive. To do this they have been forced more and more to acknowledge the importance of money, and the average Russian now worries as much about making ends meet and getting a little bit ahead as people in the United States do. But because Russians today have little or no experience with private ownership of property or paying their own way, simply holding daily life together has become a confusing and sometimes frightening task for many.

Russians are also faced with astonishing changes in their sense of their own history. The most dramatic example of this occurred in 1988, when history finals were canceled in high schools all over the nation. Government officials announced that the textbooks from which students had learned were "full of lies,"[29] and that the exams were pointless. Every day seems to bring new revelations of lies perpetrated by the Communist Party to make Soviet citizens believe that their country was prospering and that they were lucky to live there. People once revered as courageous leaders, such as the former presidents of the Soviet Union, are now defamed as their shortcomings and betrayals of the people are revealed. The revisionist atmosphere has made it difficult for people to know whom or what to trust.

On the other hand, many basic freedoms suppressed under communism such as freedom of worship, press, and speech are now permitted and have had generally positive influences on the culture. Church attendance is up and many churches are being restored. Likewise, though it may be disconcerting to learn that what one was taught in school was a lie, many, particularly younger, Russians, feel that being able to open a newspaper today and have more confidence that it contains

MCDONALD'S IN MOSCOW

No other symbol of the changes in Russia seemed to capture the attention of the Russian and American public like the opening of the first McDonald's in Moscow in 1990. Since then nearly a dozen more have opened around the city, joined by several Dunkin' Donuts and Pizza Hut franchises.

When the first McDonald's opened in Moscow, lines stretched around the block. Though today the lines are often longer than those for Lenin's tomb, the excitement has died down considerably. According to writer Ann Imse in *Insight Guide: Russia,* the initial excitement about McDonald's was not just about what in Russian sounds like "gambourgers," which customers initially thought should be smashed flat to shove in their mouths. Rather it was "the remarkable revelation that a restaurant could be clean, that service could be had in moments instead of hours and that employees could be polite and even welcoming to customers."

In the typical Russian restaurant before McDonald's arrived on the scene, Russians often had to offer a bribe to be seated and another to be served. Perhaps the company's new Russian employees were most amazed by McDonald's instruction to smile at customers. One of these employees, according to Imse, responded to the idea by saying, "people will think we're idiots."

In 1990 a McDonald's restaurant opened in Moscow.

the truth is worth the confusion and disappointment of having past lies revealed. Also, Russians today can complain openly when they do not like something about their government or their lives. Being able to criticize authority without looking over one's shoulder or speaking in whispers only to intimate friends and family is a new and exciting exercise.

Greater freedoms, however, include the corollary greater freedom to behave badly. Rates of crime against people and property have soared. In the absence of clear rules or enforceable penalties, unethical businesspeople look for opportunities to cheat customers or avoid paying taxes that would support such things as schools and health care. Overall, when Russians assess the quality of their lives, they are hard-pressed to decide whether the frightening lawlessness they now deal with, as well as their new headaches over money and lack of confidence in their government to solve the problems of daily life, are worth the new freedoms they now have.

MEETING BASIC NEEDS

One difficulty of daily life in cities and towns is housing. Even well-to-do Russians tend to live in small, often hastily built, houses or apartments. Often today roofs leak, floorboards warp, and elevators do not work. Many apartment buildings are still owned by the government, and "communal apartments" left over from Soviet days are large, some with dozens of bedrooms and a half-dozen kitchens and toilets. This way of living was encouraged by Communist leaders because most criticism of the government took place where families gathered together, and communal living made spying on one's neighbors easier. Today, because apartments can be privately owned, many buildings are being remodeled to create separate apartments, but remodeling cannot always rid a house of problems caused by poor construction. Similar situations exist in the country and smaller cities, where housing built for workers was shoddily constructed and not designed for privacy, but is still often the only option.

Rents have increased from about 5 percent to more than half of many people's income, and buying an apartment or house is out of reach for most. Even those lucky enough to live in what is considered a fairly luxurious apartment almost never have more than one bathroom or enough space for family members to have their own bedrooms.

Those at the low end of the housing spectrum face terrible hardships. For example, when the Soviet empire collapsed in Eastern Europe, more than one hundred thousand military officers and their families were sent home from posts in East Germany and Poland. Due to the serious overall housing shortage, there was no place to house them, and no work for them to do in a country that was downsizing its military at the end of the cold war. Many military families still have no permanent housing, and live in tent camps while they try to figure out what to do with their suddenly disrupted lives.

Many apartment buildings in Russia are still owned by the government.

The cost of food, like housing, has risen as well, though overall quality has not. Women, who still are responsible for most housework, carry a mesh or string bag with them at all times to stock up if they find a bargain or a rare item. In many workplaces, particularly in cities, the time-consuming task of shopping for food is shared. Because shops generally sell only one type of food—for example a fish market does not sell meat and vice versa, women form groups and spend their lunch hours standing in long lines at only one store and buying in quantity for the whole group. Thus, one woman might come back with five loaves of bread, another with several bags of vegetables,

A Russian navy officer stands inside his cramped living quarters aboard ship. Serious housing shortages exist for Russian military families.

and another with a few pounds of meat. Each goes home with her share of each product.

RELIGIOUS REVIVAL

While running errands, the women are likely to have had to find their way around the many construction sites in their city. Russia is busy restoring historic buildings and churches damaged or destroyed by the Soviets in the attempt to replace national pride with Soviet loyalty. In a country where so little seems stable or certain, restoration of churches serves at least as a symbolic reminder of a more settled time and of their country's great cultural heritage. The Communists sought to erase all influences but their own over the minds of the people. Consequently, they not only closed churches, tearing them down or converting them to other uses such as storage of food or armaments, but also harassed or banished priests and destroyed precious religious art.

Since the collapse of the Soviet Union and of communism, the Russian Orthodox Church has reemerged as a significant institution and attempted to undo the damage. Today churches are open and hold regular worship services, some complete with the all-male choirs for which Russia is famous. Near Red Square, the heart of Moscow, one beautiful cathedral that was demolished to make room for a gigantic, never completed monument to Lenin is now being reconstructed. Many Russians now make churchgoing a regular part of their lives, just as their ancestors did.

Not everyone views the revival of the church positively, however. Under communism, the Russian Orthodox Church was not entirely shut down. Some monasteries, religious communities usually in remote towns, were permitted to stay open, and many churches were saved from the wrecking ball by the efforts of church leaders. In exchange for keeping their heritage alive, church leaders had to agree to be highly visible supporters of communism. They essentially lied about the suppression of religion and did not encourage resistance or revolt the way the Catholic Church, for instance, did in Poland. Today, the Russian Orthodox Church is seen by many Russians as having sold out the people, and they want no part of it.

Many Russians are also deterred by the church's association with an extreme form of patriotism based in dislike of anything perceived as non-Russian. Today, nationalist politicians, following the lead of Vladimir Zhirinovsky, attempt to gain popularity by telling ethnic Russians that they are better than other people, and that they have a great heritage that is being corrupted by outside influences and by other ethnic groups. The Russian Orthodox Church has encouraged this chauvinism, and though it has benefited from the new freedom of religion, it has tried to suppress as non-Russian other faiths, including Judaism, both Catholic and Protestant Christianity, Islam, and Buddhism, all of which have adherents in this huge country. Thus, the religious revival has not created an open environment for Russians of all faiths, and some people are concerned that the church is evolving into a repressive rather than a liberating influence in Russian life.

The Russian Orthodox Church, while benefiting from the new religious freedom, has tried to suppress other religions.

SCHOOLS IN RUSSIA

Schools, unlike churches, were well supported under Soviet rule. Before communism only about a quarter of Russians could read and write, but by 1980, literacy rates neared 100 percent By the end of the communist era, attendance at school was required for a minimum of eight years in rural areas, but it was standard for children in cities to attend for ten or eleven years. The government dictated exactly what would be taught in all schools. History and literature focused on turning children into loyal Communists, and math and science were stressed as essential to Soviet military and industrial growth.

Under the Soviets higher education flourished as well. Whereas only twelve universities existed early in the Communist era, there were fifty-two by its end, as well as nearly a thousand technical colleges. Education, including at universities, was free, and women and men were equally encouraged to pursue higher education. In fact, by the 1980s there were more women with university degrees than men. University educations also tended to focus on very narrow skills and knowledge felt to be helpful to the Soviet state.

Today, schooling has changed considerably. Many private high schools stress specific subjects such as the arts or in-

Education, now struggling in a market economy, was well supported under the Communist form of government.

RETEACHING HISTORY

History textbooks used in Russia until the end of the Soviet era were based on a book called *The Short Course,* the Stalin-approved version of history. After all high school history exams in the country were canceled in 1988, work began on a new curriculum. However, even today efforts to change what is taught have run into several difficulties.

The first is that many teachers are comfortable with the old way and with the old "facts." According to one teacher quoted in Hedrick Smith's *The New Russians,* teachers trained in the Communist era "have not been taught to analyze . . . They just accept. If they get a textbook, *any* textbook, they will teach whatever is in it." Some teachers, however, resist change for other reasons. They feel that the emphasis on the negative is now too strong. Another teacher quoted by Smith argues that "indoctrination in citizenship—that's my most important task. Basically that means, despite all our problems, love your motherland and its people and respect their achievement." Though she does not believe children should be lied to, she feels schools should try to instill in young people an image of something positive and believes "too much criticism is dangerous."

Even those who feel strongly that the errors of the past must be emphasized cannot always agree on the facts. For example, historians do not agree on how to count the victims of Stalin. Some argue that only those directly killed should be counted, but others feel that victims of starvation and other hardships caused by his policies should be included in the total. Another argument has arisen over whether what is often called the Red Terror, the era of violent suppression in the effort to create the Communist state, should be said to have started with Lenin or with Stalin. This is a particularly sticky question because though Stalin has become a villain as a result of his murderous reign, Lenin's acts of violence have to this point been downplayed because he is still viewed as a visionary leader, a national hero, and the founder of his country. To discredit Lenin would, some think, call into question everything about communism and cast the entire twentieth century as a big mistake.

ternational studies, and can be both expensive and exclusive. Public schools have been hard hit by the downturn in the Russian economy. Tax dollars that would support schools are often uncollected, and the result is dilapidated schools, inadequate teaching materials, and poorly paid and demoralized teachers. Even though Russian winters are long and extremely cold, by the end of the Soviet era, over one-fifth of the public schools had no central heating and 40 percent had no indoor toilets. The situation has not improved since.

University education is still free for anyone whose grades are high enough to be admitted, but funding decreases have caused quality to slip. Many applicants turn to private colleges, which charge fees and which specialize in career skills such as computer programming, medical assistance, and the performing arts. Financial aid is not widely available, and thus many students cannot attend these colleges. Overall the participation of women in higher education has fallen substantially. The Soviet emphasis on universal workforce participation has been lost, and there is now a stronger expectation that women choose family life over careers.

DIET AND DRINK

The Russian diet is heavy in starches and emphasizes meat whenever it is available. Fresh vegetables are served in small quantities or as an ingredient in a meat dish. Often the meat is of low quality, and one travel writer has joked that the Russian method for slaughtering poultry is starvation. Traditional Russian dishes are not actually very popular, at least in the cities, where Western food is preferred. Though enough food is available to feed everyone, there is still nowhere near the variety of cuisines or ingredients found in the West. Because what is most often available tends to be high in calories, slim Russian youth usually begin putting on weight in their twenties and often become quite stout by the time they are middle-aged. Special diets are difficult to follow, and because there are still not enough grocery stores to create much competition or specialization, Russians by and large have to eat what they can find.

Russians rarely encounter a problem finding vodka, and they consume it in enormous quantities. One recent survey of consumer purchases concluded that the amount of vodka consumed each year averages forty bottles for every man, woman, and child in the country. It is considered sociable to drink until passing out, and it is not considered sociable to refuse. Alcohol consumption skyrocketed during the Brezhnev era. During the 1980s it was widely available and very cheap, some say, as a means of distracting Russians from the many problems caused by the failing Communist system. The result today is a population with a serious drinking problem, particularly among men. Largely as a result of alcoholism, the life expectancy for men has dropped below sixty years. Disease and accidents such as drowning account for much of this. Even former President Boris Yeltsin was famous for appearing drunk in public and for missing official appearances due to hangovers. With more opportunities for travel and trade, other street drugs have also become easily available, but by far the largest societal problem is alcohol abuse.

HEALTH AND HEALTH CARE

Under communism free health care was available for all Soviet citizens. The fact that any Soviet citizen could see a doctor, get medicine, and even be hospitalized entirely free of charge was one the Party's proudest achievements. However, according to author Michael Kort, "By the 1980s, Soviet health care, like the rest of the Soviet system, was rife with corruption and problems."[30] Some hospitals even lacked running water and functioning sewage systems, and thus could not enforce basic sanitary practices even for surgeries. Also, according to Kort, "Doctors were poorly trained or completely incompetent."[31] All of these factors contributed to the fact that life expectancy actually began to drop in the Soviet Union in the 1970s, when it began to rise in other European nations.

Like much else about the command economy, health care soon functioned on bribery. According to Kort, "By the 1980s, most people had to bribe their way into a good hospital and then pay for everything from a doctor's care to basic drugs." These drugs as well as basic supplies often had to be bought on the black market because the government had failed to supply them to pharmacies, clinics, and hospitals in adequate amounts. Doctors took bribes primarily because their "pitifully low"[32] salaries made the chance for a little money on the side too tempting to resist. Thus, despite government claims to the contrary, there were really two health care systems operating in Soviet Russia— the free (and dangerously inadequate) one and the expensive, bribery-driven one.

Today, according to Daniel Yergin and Thane Gustafson, "Things the West takes for granted, such as disposable syringes, are not readily available throughout Russia."[33] Simply increasing medical supplies will not solve the problem because hospital and clinic buildings need substantial repairs. One minister of health recently estimated that it would take more than twice as much money as the country now spends on public health to make the system even adequate. The country does not have the money to do this, in part because it cannot collect all the taxes it is owed, but even if it had the money, it has no history of running a truly functioning state health system because the previous one was not as good as it pretended to be. Doctors can now legally and openly supplement their incomes by opening private practices, but not many people can afford private care. Thus, most doctors still work at least part-time for the state in dilapidated, inadequate facilities for poor pay—a situation that is likely to continue.

Evidence of the growing health crisis was an epidemic of diphtheria in 1992 and 1993. The outbreak started in Moscow but soon spread across Russia. One cause of the epidemic was the fact that the inoculation program for children had broken down, and children were not receiving shots on schedule; another contributing factor was the poor living conditions of many Russians. Also, according to Daniel Yergin and Thane Gustafson, "The growing incidence of preventable infectious disease such as diphtheria and cholera suggests a population under stress, malnourished, and increasingly vulnerable to illness, as well as a health system that is breaking down."[34]

LIVING WITHOUT LAWS

Law and order is also breaking down across the board, in business as well as in private life. A hidden and illegal economic system, or black market, enabled people to buy and sell things. This kept Russians alive in years when the government could not even keep food on store shelves, but because black market activity was hidden from government authorities, the judicial system was not involved. People who cheated in the black market might be beaten up or killed, but they would definitely not be taken to court. Thus, when communism fell, no one really looked to the government to protect sellers or buyers when suddenly businesses were out in the open. Also, new store and company owners lack experience making binding business deals, using the law to settle business disputes, or following laws regarding fair treatment of employees. At any rate, in Russia, according to Hedrick Smith, "the fuzzy legal situation makes it hard for anyone to know for sure he is following the rules";[35] likewise, no one is sure who has power to enforce them. For example, businesses often simply do not pay their employees. Some people, including government employees such as teachers, go for months without receiving a paycheck, but unpaid workers have no formal channels to file claims, and lack clear legal protections.

Because Russians have little experience owning property, legal concepts regarding theft or damage that Westerners take for granted are not well developed in Russia. Under communism, if a farmer drove a tractor into a ditch, fixing the broken axle would have been the government's problem. Now that the tractor could belong to a neighbor, concepts of responsibility for property must be developed. However, even if the laws were

clear, bribery is still so rampant that, according to one bank executive interviewed and quoted by Pulitzer prize–winning author David Remnick, "government officials practically have a price list hanging on the wall."[36]

Because people have little confidence that the law and the courts can protect their property or their rights, they have turned increasingly to "protection services." In fact, according to David Remnick, the legal system is so ineffective that many prominent and wealthy businesspeople think it "better to hire an assassin and a bodyguard"[37] than rely on the law. One recent development illustrates the extent to which lawlessness pervades the daily lives of Russians. In Moscow, people with nice apartments have recently become attractive targets of kidnappers. They are tortured and threatened with death if they do not sign over their apartments to their abductor. Sometimes they are killed anyway after they have signed the necessary documents. Because the documents are legal, and because the police lack the resources or the clear authority to pursue these criminals, people can do nothing about the loss of their homes. Of course, a home owner who fears this has only to accept the services of a protection service, perhaps

Many Russians are hard hit by promarket economic reforms. An expression of their frustration appears in this graffiti.

even the same individuals threatening the kidnapping, to avoid any further problems and to keep the property "safe."

Owning private property or having money in a culture that lacks adequate personal protections has created many other previously unheard-of crimes. Both crimes and the protection racket have become a very profitable enterprise for the Russian mafia. The Russian mafia is a large collection of competing gangs that, in addition to selling protection, control the drug trade and run other illegal operations across Russia and abroad. They operate much like American organized crime, with one key difference: In Russia there is no doubt that high-ranking officials are deeply involved. In exchange for gifts and profit, they have ensured that mafia activities go unpunished. In fact, mafia criminals can be almost certain that if they are punished at all it will be in the form of a hit by another gang.

LEISURE

Life in Russia is not all violence and misery, however. Many Russian city dwellers lease small plots of land outside the city on which they build retreats called dachas. They spend as much time as they can in the summer at their dachas, then close them up for the winter. Dachas are a form of holiday from everyday life, although because the goal is usually to grow and preserve as much produce as possible to last through the winter, dacha summers are rarely a holiday from work. Dachas of the rich can be gated mansions, but those of the middle class tend to be fairly primitive, often with outhouses rather than indoor plumbing.

During the Communist era, when travel outside the Soviet Union was severely restricted, resorts built on the Black Sea and other places provided a place for Soviet citizens to take free annual vacations. These resorts still attract Russian citizens today, many of whose vacations are paid for by their employer. Russians are fond of a wide range of sports both as observers and participants, and this focus, as well as rigorous, state-supported sports programs, has contributed to their long history of dominance in the modern winter and summer Olympics. Intellectual activities are also prized. Russia is a nation of readers, and public transportation such as buses are sometime jokingly referred to as reading rooms. Chess is a national obsession, and Russia has produced many of the world's greatest players.

Russians relax in a hot spring.

   More freedom to attend church, read formerly forbidden
books, and spend personal money on hobbies gives Russians
an increased sense of control over their leisure time, if not
the rest of their daily lives. This in turn gives many Russians
hope that even greater enjoyment of other aspects of life may
soon lie ahead.

6

ARTS & ENTERTAINMENT

At the height of World War II, between 1941 and 1943, St. Petersburg (then known as Leningrad) fell under siege by the Nazis. Food and supplies were cut off along all routes except by truck or sled crossing the frozen Gulf of Finland. Electricity and the public water supply were cut for more than five hundred days, including most of two bitterly cold winters. Nazi tanks and bombers frequently shelled the city, killing and wounding many thousands and keeping everyone in a constant state of fright. Hundreds of thousands were starving, and there seemed to be no end in sight.

At the height of the suffering from the blockade, which ultimately cost nearly half a million lives, Russian composer Dmitry Shostakovich completed his Seventh Symphony. Residents of St. Petersburg flocked to the concert hall to see Shostakovich himself conduct the premiere. Many orchestra members were off at war or dead, but with their colleagues' instruments lovingly laid on their empty chairs, the remaining orchestra played. Amid shelling around the concert hall, the hungry and war-torn audience listened in tears. It was the first concert in months, a new work by one of their own. More than that, it was a reminder that art can make life endurable, and that despite their current hardships, they were still part of a great culture.

ARTS IN THE SOVIET ERA

The story of the siege of Leningrad and Shostakovich's Seventh Symphony illustrates the power that the arts held and still hold in Russians' lives. Life without music and something to read is unimaginable for most Russians.

Shostakovich's career also illustrates another fact about Russian arts in the twentieth century: the Communists were more than willing to support the arts as long as the arts supported communism. Shostakovich, for example, released his opera *Lady Macbeth of Mtsensk* in 1934, to rave reviews. Two years later, however, after Stalin came to a performance, an editorial entitled "Chaos Instead of Music" appeared in the government-controlled newspaper *Pravda*, and Shostakovich endured similar attacks from then on about almost everything he wrote. To Stalin, Russian music should sound cheerful and melodic, reflecting a happy people on their way to creating a worker's paradise. Music that struck Stalin as insufficiently grand or upbeat was, to his suspicious mind, an attack against communism. Shostakovich's Seventh Symphony was tolerated only because Stalin realized that the people badly needed a morale boost during the war. As soon as the war was over, he once again viciously denounced Shostakovich.

Shostakovich's experience was typical of that of artists of all categories. Many were, like himself, committed Communists, but pursued artistic visions that extended beyond making political statements. Some responded to state controls by immigrating or defecting to the United States or Western Europe, but many writers and artists remained, resigned to work in obscurity, or conforming their art to Soviet expectations.

Russian composer Dmitry Shostakovich wrote his Seventh Symphony during the height of World War II.

VLAD LISTYEV

By the mid-1990s, murders were an everyday occurrence in Moscow and rarely made headlines. However, when thirty-eight-year-old television personality Vlad Listyev was gunned down outside his Moscow apartment in March 1995, his death unleashed an unprecedented public outcry of grief and rage. According to David Remnick in *Resurrection,* "After Yeltsin, he was the most famous man in the country—and probably the most popular." Remnick adds that "broadcasters on the evening news announced Listyev's murder with the sort of gravity . . . accorded to the passing of a king." Tens of thousands of people lined the funeral route, and over 10 million more watched on television.

Vladislav Listyev was a young radio star in 1987 when he was invited to join a new television show, *Vzglyad,* meaning "glance," which, in the words of Hedrick Smith in *The New Russians,* was a "blend of cool informality, hot rock, and the most modern gimmickry on Soviet TV, a brassy weekly magazine show combining *Nightline, 60 Minutes,* and MTV." From *Vzglyad,* Listyev moved on to create new shows modeled after American game and talk shows such as *Wheel of Fortune* and *Larry King Live,* all with himself as host. He was young, handsome, sophisticated, and rich at a time when most other television personalities were none of those things, and he grew into a genuine idol and role model for many in the new Russia.

Listyev, however, was more than a pretty face and a good dresser. He was also a shrewd businessman, forming a production company to make new shows and becoming one of the first to sell air time for commercials on his shows. He eventually became general producer and manager of Ostankino, the largest television station in Russia, the job he held at the time of his death.

Theories abounded as to motive for the murder, ranging from a jealous lover, to a business deal gone bad, to a government plot, but the truth will probably never be known, because in the crime-ridden Russia of today any of those things—or a hundred more—could be true.

Vlad Listyev, a popular television personality, was gunned down outside his Moscow apartment.

Those who "went along" were treated very well. Favored artists were given special privileges such as membership in exclusive artists' supper clubs, where they were fed as well as Party bosses. They were paid better than professionals such as doctors, and they always had the resources and supplies they needed to create new works. As long as they conformed to Party expectations, their new works, whether a symphony, a novel, or an exhibition of paintings, were treated as the greatest achievement of the age and the artists were celebrated. True artistic greatness, however, is original and daring—not traits the Soviet government wanted to encourage. Today, with the exception of Shostakovich and his fellow composer Sergey Prokofiev (most famous among young audiences for "Peter and the Wolf,") those government- sponsored composers, writers, painters, and other artists have faded into oblivion.

Cellist Mstislav Rostropovich conducts a symphony in a free concert in Moscow's Red Square in 1993.

MUSIC AND LITERATURE UNDER GLASNOST

"With glasnost," according to art scholar Rosamund Bartlett, "came an explosion of Soviet cultural life, as artists and writers were allowed to travel freely to the West for the first time, and previously forbidden works were published and performed."[38] Exiled artists, such as cellist Mstislav Rostropovich and pianist

Vladimir Ashkenazy, made dazzling "welcome home" tours, and neglected composers such as Alfred Schnittke began to attract the recognition they deserved. A much wider range of music—both Russian and Western—became available, as the government was no longer determined to see the West as corrupt and Russian artists as little more than homegrown Party cheerleaders.

In literature, the immediate result of glasnost was to bring banned books to the public's attention. Novels such as Boris Pasternak's *Dr. Zhivago* and Vladimir Nabokov's *Lolita* were better known in the West than in their own country, where both were banned. The best-known Russian writer of the late Soviet era both within Russia and abroad was Nobel prize–winner Aleksandr Solzhenitsyn. Some of his works, such as his 1962 short novel *One Day in the Life of Ivan Denisovich*, about life in Stalin's labor camps, had been praised in Khrushchev's Soviet Union both because Stalin was officially out of favor and as a means of rebutting worldwide criticism about Communist censorship. Solzhenitsyn went too far, however, with *The Gulag Archipelago*. His factual exposé of the many-tentacled penal system of Soviet labor camps earned him deportation and exile from his country until 1994.

Solzhenitsyn, Nabokov, and others had earned international fame by being published outside the Soviet Union, but some banned works had never been published at all. "New" works such as Yevgeny Zamyatin's *We*, actually written in the 1920s, were being read by Russians for the first time in the 1990s. Zamyatin's accurate and frightening depiction of a totalitarian state gave many Russians pause, realizing that what Zamyatin had been trying to warn them about had indeed come to pass. Other newly published works by contemporary writers were encouraged by the establishment in 1992 of an annual national prize for literature, which included what amounted to an astronomical cash award of around $20,000. The first recipient was Mark Kharitonov, author of a novel entitled *Lines of Fate*. Kharitonov won, in part, because his novel was not overtly political. It did not denounce one way of thinking and living or praise another. It was simply good literature, sending the message that in the new Russia, quality would be the measure of an artist.

Though Russia is a nation of readers, the new support for good writing has not resulted in a great deal of new, high-quality work for Russians to read. First, publishing houses face the same problem as other privatizing businesses: lack of money. Very few presses can afford to put resources into publishing unknown writers. Most writers turn to journals such as *Ogonyok,* which had reached a circulation of around 3 million by the 1990s, for exposure.

Second, under decades of communism, just as the quality of books Russians could read dropped dramatically, so had Russian reading tastes. According to Vladimir Sorokin, a contemporary Russian writer, "it will take a long time for the present generation to tire of Stock Exchange news and James Bond novels, and start to want literature. It is not [the writer's] time," Sorokin adds. "No one needs him."[39] Of course, not all agree with Sorokin. In June 1999 millions of people all across Russia participated in a lavish, multimillion- dollar bicentennial celebration of Russian poet, Aleksandr Pushkin—a sign that love of literature is most certainly not dead in post-Communist Russia.

VISUAL ARTS IN THE NEW RUSSIA

Of all art forms, those most thoroughly suppressed under the Soviets were painting and the other visual arts. Art in the twentieth century broke away from traditional and realistic ways of presenting subjects, in favor of more abstract compositions. Colors and shapes were often distorted, sometimes beyond the point of recognition, and it was generally difficult to understand what, if anything, the artist was trying to say. The Soviet leaders hated this abstraction, and non-realist Russian painters rarely had opportunities to exhibit their work. On one of these rare occasions, Soviet leader Nikita Khrushchev got into a shouting match with a Russian painter, using the profanity to express his opinion of the low quality of the work in the exhibit.

Because the state controlled everything, the disapproval of the Party chief was far more significant than in the West where the opinion of the president about art means little at all. Though some artists found their reputations boosted among other artists by Party disapproval, they could not earn a living through their art as long as they remained in Russia. Most who achieved international fame in the twentieth century, such as Vasily Kandinsky and Marc Chagall, did so from abroad, and those who stayed home settled for obscurity. According to art specialist Ivan Samarine, by the 1930s, "all art was . . . subjugated to the Party, and this situation remained, with a few underground exceptions, until the era of perestroika."[40]

ALEKSANDR PUSHKIN, SUPERSTAR

On June 6, 1999, people all over Russia celebrated the two hundredth anniversary of the birth of Aleksandr Pushkin, the country's most popular poet. The Russian Federation spent the equivalent of over 2 million dollars on parties, fireworks, concerts, and other celebrations in each of the eleven time zones of the country. For months building up to the June 6 event, Russian television had featured a countdown to the anniversary. Every day a Russian citizen read a few lines of Pushkin and announced how many days were left until his birthday. The readers were ordinary citizens for the most part—schoolchildren, secretaries, firefighters, military officers, and street people.

All the fuss was for a poet who has continued to strike a chord with Russians even today. Pushkin is said to have been the first to recognize and highlight the beauty of the Russian language, but his independence and rebellious nature also made him a hero. He was proud of the fact that he was part African, the offspring of one of Peter the Great's black servants, and this ethnic heritage is one of the things that gives him a special mystique in Russia. He died at age thirty-eight in a duel with a French officer whom he suspected of having an affair with his wife.

Pushkin's bicentennial was commemorated by 109 hours of nationwide Pushkin-related television coverage. In Moscow, world-famous tenor Placido Domingo gave a concert in honor of Pushkin's contribution to opera—the poem *Eugene Onegin*, which was interpreted as opera by Peter Tchaikovsky. Boris Yeltsin presided over the awarding of a new Pushkin prize to twenty-eight people who had made contributions to the arts in Russia. In St. Petersburg, torrential rains marred the celebration a bit, but most participants, some sporting new Pushkin haircuts, simply munched on their commemorative Pushkin pickles and Pushkin chocolates, well lubricated by Pushkin commemorative vodka, and let the party go on.

A bronze sculpture in St. Petersburg commemorates Aleksandr Pushkin, Russia's most popular poet.

By the time Mikhail Gorbachev introduced glasnost, a stereotype of the Russian painter as a "poor, unshaven, misunderstood genius" had evolved, and the first painters to emerge in the 1980s cultivated this image of great souls suffering for their art. However, soon others were rolling their eyes at what they perceived as the phoniness of this image. A group of painters who called their association Mitki shunned the stereotype of the suffering artist in favor of its opposite. According to Valera Katsuba, Mitki members "stopped shaving, became fat, threw back glasses of cheap vodka and smoked cheap cigarettes"[41] all as a statement about their loss of belief in just about everything, from underground heroes to Party chiefs. Their behavior rather than their art gained them their reputation, striking a chord with disenchanted Russians everywhere.

In the 1980s every kind of art seemed to emerge all at once. Painters set up easels on the streets or drew in chalk on the pavement to make a little money. More serious artists did more daring things to establish their reputations. Ivan Movsesyan, for example, hung painted canvases from a bridge outside the Hermitage, the state museum in St. Petersburg. Another artist, Sergey Bugayev, who calls himself Africa, cut a door in the legs of a huge statue of a Soviet worker in St. Petersburg, climbed into the hollow space inside, and invited people to join him. These acts, which might seem like no more than attention-getting pranks in the West, amazed Russians because only a few years before such acts would have been tantamount to suicide.

The art scene in St. Petersburg today retains some of this irreverent, impromptu feeling, but Moscow's art scene is characterized by more concentrated efforts to make art pay. Moscow art galleries track carefully what is popular in the West and what wealthy patrons are likely to buy. However, few artists and galleries are able to make ends meet, because the Russian government, sensing a way to make money, heavily taxes paintings sold and shipped abroad. In some documented cases the tax has been 600 percent more than the buyer paid for the art. Some efforts are underway, such as the organization called A-Ya in St. Petersburg, to stop this exploitation, which threatens to kill the enthusiasm of new Russian artists for developing and marketing their talents.

MAKING THE SCENE, RUSSIAN STYLE

Artists such as Africa and Monroe, so named because of his habit of appearing in drag as Marilyn Monroe, developed a Russian version of a rave party that has been popular since the early 1990s. Today companies such as Blokk, MX, and Tanzpol arrange raves, often in settings such as large public swimming pools, parks, and palaces. A phenomenon known as "Saturday night clubs" has also evolved. These events are similar to raves but are held at the same places every Saturday night. In recent years the mafia has moved in on rave organizers, demanding up to 30 percent of the gate. It remains to be seen what impact this will have on the rave and nightclub scene.

Rock bands in Russia tend to be very loud, fashioning themselves after punk, goth, and heavy metal styles of the West. Few are known at all outside Russia, in part because they have not found something they can do better or differently enough to attract an audience in the West, and in part because Russian recording and production studios are far inferior. Only recently, for instance, have Russian bands been able to produce video clips, and many find it impossible even to get a studio recording made at all. Still, young people flock to nightclubs to hear the latest groups, who become popular more by word of mouth than by recordings.

MEDIA POLITICS

During the Communist era, all media were heavily censored. Only a few newspapers and three television stations served the whole nation in the 1970s and 1980s—all owned and controlled by the government. One Brezhnev-era joke involves a person turning on the television to channel one and seeing Brezhnev droning on about some Party achievement. The viewer switches to channel two and sees the same thing. On channel three, an army officer points a gun and tells the viewer to return to channel one immediately.

Television and other media changed—although slowly—under glasnost. Today, a wide range of newspapers is published, airing a wide range of views. None is as widely read as it would have been before the era of television, however. Some argue that censorship of the press had largely ended even before glasnost because the government realized the negative image it would incur by shutting down papers hardly anyone read was not worth it. By the 1970s television,

not newspapers, was already the main source of information for the vast majority of the Russian public.

However, even today there are still only a handful of television stations. Several are owned by the state and a few are independently owned, although still tightly regulated. Though there is more freedom to report negative news and poke fun at government figures, exercising that freedom still seems risky to many, particularly older journalists. One producer interviewed by journalist Hedrick Smith commented that "we try to argue with our superiors. We tell them 'We . . . will air our show.' But we still have this feeling of fear. . . . We ask ourselves, 'Can we do it or can't we do it? Will it be allowed or not?'" In the same group interview, a young reporter disagreed, saying "not everyone is afraid. . . . We have an opportunity to make basic changes, to try to change the political system."[42]

Whether television will be a means of changing the political system no longer seems a matter of debate, but it probably will not happen in the way envisioned by the second reporter. The value of television as a shaper of public opinion is clear to politicians, and it is their access to and control of the air waves that is

Russian rock bands tend to be very loud, fashioning themselves after Western-style musicians.

CHECHNYA: RUSSIA'S FIRST LIVING-ROOM WAR

Television is not only the way most Russians get the news, but is for many the only available form of entertainment. Thus, when television stations began coverage in December 1994 of the Chechens' battle with the Russian army over Chechnya's declaration of independence, almost everyone in Russia was watching. Chechnya became for Russians the equivalent of Vietnam for Americans—the first time that death and destruction inflicted by their own government was reviewed in agonizing detail every night on the news.

If Russians watched the government-owned station, Ostankino, they would have seen the Russian army portrayed, according to Pulitzer prize–winning reporter David Remnick in *Resurrection*, as "a friendly force come to liberate the local population from its evil local leaders and guerrillas." If they watched NTV, the new, privately financed and thus more independent station, they would have seen, according to Remnick, "a slaughterhouse." The capital city, Grozny, had been nearly leveled by Russian army bombardment, which at its height reached four thousand detonations an hour. Remnick, an eyewitness, comments that he "could not quite believe it possible" that a city could be so senselessly destroyed even after it was clear the only people remaining were defenseless civilians, many of them children. The slaughter was not confined to Russians killing Chechens, however. According to Remnick, "The Russian force—undermanned, confused, and egged on by a president [Yeltsin] . . . who insisted on a quick victory—trudged through knee-high mud and blinding winter fogs and was met by well-trained guerrilla forces." The Chechens ambushed tanks, blew up Russian troops with grenades, and picked off Russian soldiers with sniper fire. All this was on the news, to the humiliation of Yeltsin and the defense minister, who had predicted a complete victory over the Chechens in two hours.

To minimize the damage, Yeltsin's ministers even briefly considered blowing up NTV's transmitter. In the end they settled for the tried-and-true Soviet approach: intimidation. NTV officials were called to a conference at which they were told to tone down their reporting or be put out of business. Nevertheless, Boris Yeltsin was never able to recover his image as a man of the people. According to Remnick, "No matter what good he had done in the past ten years, he would not undo this. He could fire all the ministers he wanted, but it would not lift the blame from him."

the hot issue today. Television is credited with influencing the outcome of the 1991 and 1993 elections, not by thoughtful debates over issues, but by tactics many observers considered unethical. Condom-and vodka-wielding candidate Vladimir Zhirinovsky, for example, had an instinctive feel for the "sound bite," and built his appeal not by a well-thought-out political program but by quick slogans. Boris Yeltsin is widely believed to have stolen the 1993 election by a last-minute negative television campaign against his Communist opponent. Today, with government control over television looser than it has ever been, all parties are worried about elections in the future. If the overall chaos in the government is any indication, it is likely that politicians will do or say just about anything on television to influence voters, and the election results will thus be based on misinformation and gimmicks, not on issues or platforms.

Boris Yeltsin's establishment in July 1999 of a new ministry for the media was an attempt to address the potential misuse of television in the upcoming elections. This new ministry was set up to oversee and provide fair and equal treatment for various candidates in the upcoming elections. Yeltsin's opponents doubt that his real goal was the fair, open, and democratic election process he claimed to want, and it remains to be seen whether a ministry appointed by Yeltsin will really give fair coverage to politicians whose views Yeltsin and Putin do not like. Nevertheless, the establishment of a ministry is a sign that politicians are beginning to realize that their new freedoms bring with them the obligation to behave responsibly.

When Mikhail Gorbachev first introduced the ideas of glasnost and perestroika, and Boris Yeltsin first began talking of democracy, Russians had very little idea what either man meant. The political troubles both men soon experienced indicate they did not realize the massive and far-reaching impact the fundamental changes they proposed would have on their society. To many Russians, freedom meant doing whatever one wanted, and in those first heady months, when the repressions of the past seemed suddenly lifted, Russia embarked on a chaotic journey from which it has not yet emerged strong and stable. However, as the first full post-Communist decade comes to an end, the old saying that only Russians can conquer Russia rings particularly true. On the other hand, only Russians can build Russia as well, and the next few years are likely to reveal what kind of a Russia that will be.

FACTS ABOUT THE RUSSIAN FEDERATION

Official Name: Russian Federation/Rosiyskaya Federatsiya, or in brief, Russia/Rossiya

Type of Government: Federation, established August 24, 1991, of member countries of the former Soviet Union

Capital: Moscow

Administrative Divisions: Autonomous republics: 21

Oblasts: 49

Territories: 6

Districts: 10

FEDERAL GOVERNMENT STRUCTURE

Chief of State/President: Vladimir Putin

Head of Government/Prime Minister:

Vladimir Putin	1999
Sergei Stepashin	1999
Yevgeny Primakov	1998–1999
Victor Chernomyrdin	1998 (acting)
Sergei Kirienko	1998
Victor Chernomyrdin	1992–1998
Yegor Gaidar	1992
Boris Yeltsin	1991–1992

Legislative Branch: Bicameral (two-house) Federal Assembly

Federation Council: 178 seats (2 from each of the 89 federal units, filled by top government leaders from the unit)

Duma: 450 seats (Half elected by popular vote in small units having one representative. For other half, parties that receive more than 5 percent of the popular vote nationwide receive an equal percentage of the 225 remaining seats, which they fill with people from their party's list of candidates.)

Judicial Branch: All judges are appointed for life by the federation council on recommendation of president. Three court levels:

Constitutional court

Supreme Court

Superior Court of Arbitration

POPULATION (1998 OFFICIAL ESTIMATES)

Total Population: 146,861,022

Age Structure:

0–14 years:	20%
15–64 years:	68%
65 and over:	12% (male/female ratio: 1/2.4)

Population Growth Rate: minus 0.31%

Birth Rate: 9.57 births/1000 population

Total Fertility Rate: 1.34 children born per woman. Estimated 6 abortions per woman due to lack of available birth control methods or education.

Death Rate: 14.89 deaths/1000 population

Net Emigration Rate: 2.21/ 1000 population

Life Expectancy:

total population:	64.97 years
males:	58.61 years
females:	71.64 years

Ethnic Groups:

Russian:	81.5%
Tatar:	3.8%
Ukrainian:	3%
Chuvash:	1%
Other:	10.7%

Religions: Russian Orthodox (majority), Islam, Judaism, Roman Catholicism, Protestantism, Buddhism, other

Literacy Rate (percentage of people 15 and over who can read and write): male: 100%

female: 97%

GEOGRAPHY

Total Area: 17 million square kilometers (6.5 million square miles). Approximately 1.8 times the size of United States

Bordering Countries: Azerbaijan, Belarus, China, Estonia, Finland, Georgia, Kazakhstan, North Korea, Latvia, Lithuania, Mongolia, Norway, Poland, Ukraine

Terrain and Climate: Broad plains and low hills west of Urals (the traditional dividing line between European Russia and Asian Russia). Vast evergreen forests and tundra in Siberia, uplands and mountains in south. Climate ranging from subarctic in north and east to subtropical (above freezing) along the Black Sea. Generally cool to cold, with short, warm summers, and long, extremely cold winters in most regions.

Natural Resources: Major deposits of oil, natural gas, coal, and other minerals. Large timber forests. Permafrost makes developing resources difficult in north. Lack of sea ports and arable soil despite large size of country

Environmental Issues: pollution of air and soil, deforestation, soil erosion, radioactive contamination

ECONOMY (1997 FIGURES)

Monetary Unit: ruble

Rate of Inflation:

1996	22%
1997	11%

Double-digit inflation expected through 2002, exact rate uncertain due to uncertain value of ruble

Government Budget:

revenues:	US$59 billion
expenditures:	US$70 billion

Foreign Debt: US$135 billion

Gross Domestic Product (1997 figures): US$692 billion

Gross Domestic Product (real growth rate): 0.4%

Gross Domestic Product (per capita purchasing power): US$4,700

Gross Domestic Product by Sector:

agriculture:	7%
industry:	39%
services:	54%

Unemployment: 9%, plus substantial underemployment

Industries: manufacturing (transportation and heavy equipment), mining, medical and scientific instruments

Agriculture: grain, sugar, beets, meat, dairy products, sunflower seeds

Exports: petroleum, natural gas, wood, metals, chemicals, military and civilian heavy equipment

Imports: machinery and equipment, consumer goods, medicines, meat, grain

Major Trading Partners: Europe, North America, Japan, developing countries

Principal Exports to Russia from the United States: meat, machinery, tobacco

Principal Imports from Russia to the United States: aluminum, precious stones and metals, iron, steel

NOTES

INTRODUCTION: THE CHANGING GIANT

1. Robert Service, *A History of Twentieth-Century Russia.* Cambridge, MA: Harvard University Press, 1997, p. xxxiv.

2. Daniel Yergin and Thane Gustafson, *Russia 2010—and What It Means for the World.* New York: Vintage Books, 1995, p. 121.

3. Quoted in Yergin and Gustafson, *Russia 2010,* p. 21.

CHAPTER 1: BUILDING COMMUNISM

4. John Channon, *The Penguin Historical Atlas of Russia.* London: Penguin Books, 1995, p. 80.

5. Channon, *The Penguin Historical Atlas of Russia,* p. 93.

6. Rowlinson Carter, "The Last Tsars," *Insight Guide: Russia.* Singapore: APA Publications, 1998, p. 46.

7. Channon, *The Penguin Historical Atlas of Russia,* p. 100.

CHAPTER 2: THE SOVIET UNION: 1922–1991

8. Quoted in Brian Moynahan, *The Russian Century: A History of the Last Hundred Years.* New York: Random House, 1994, p. 106.

9. Quoted in Moynahan, *The Russian Century,* p. 106.

10. Adam Hochschild, *The Unquiet Ghost: Russians Remember Stalin.* New York: Penguin Books USA, 1994, p. xv.

11. Quoted in Moynahan, *The Russian Century,* p. 210.

12. Moynahan, *The Russian Century,* p. 211.

13. Quoted in Moynahan, *The Russian Century,* p. 215.

14. Ann Imse, "The Perils of Perestroika," *Insight Guide: Russia,* p. 58.

15. Imse, "The Perils of Perestroika," *Insight Guide: Russia,* p. 59.

CHAPTER 3: RESTRUCTURING THE ECONOMY

16. Quoted in Yergin and Gustafson, *Russia 2010,* p. 58.

17. David Remnick, *Lenin's Tomb: The Last Days of the Soviet Empire.* New York: Vintage Books, 1994, p. 186.

18. Hedrick Smith, *The New Russians.* New York: Avon Books, 1990, p. 246.

19. Donald N. Jensen, "How Russia Is Ruled: Continuity of Elites," Radio Free Europe/Radio Liberty, 1998, www.rferl.org, p. 2.

20. Jensen, "How Russia Is Ruled," p. 2.

21. Economist Intelligence Unit, "Russian Federation," September 9, 1998, www.eiu.com.

CHAPTER 4: POLITICS AND NATIONHOOD

22. Imse, "The Perils of Perestroika," *Insight Guide: Russia,* p. 60.

23. Imse, "The Perils of Perestroika," *Insight Guide: Russia,* p. 60

24. "The Constitution of the Russian Federation of Dec. 12, 1993," *Russia Today,* June 30, 1999, http://www.russiatoday.com .

25. Jensen, "How Russia Is Ruled," p. 2.

26. Jensen, "How Russia Is Ruled," p. 3.

27. Jensen, "How Russia Is Ruled," p. 6.

28. David Remnick, *Resurrection: The Struggle for a New Russia.* New York: Vintage Books, 1998, p. 260.

CHAPTER 5: CHANGES IN DAILY LIFE

29. Smith, *The New Russians,* p. 106.

30. Michael Kort, *Russia.* New York: Facts On File, 1995, p. 124.

31. Kort, *Russia,* p. 124.

32. Kort, *Russia,* p. 124.

33. Yergin and Gustafson, *Russia 2010,* p. 227.

34. Yergin and Gustafson, *Russia 2010,* p. 227.

35. Smith, *The New Russians,* p. 284.

36. Quoted in Remnick, *Resurrection,* p, 356.

37. Remnick, *Resurrection,* p. 256.

CHAPTER 6: ARTS & ENTERTAINMENT

38. Rosamund Bartlett, "The Music Makers," *Insight Guide: Russia,* p. 129.

39. Quoted in Rowlinson Carter, "Literature," *Insight Guide: Russia,* p. 120.

40. Ivan Samarine, "Art: From Icons to the Avant-Garde," *Insight Guide: Russia,* p. 111.

41. Valera Katsuba, "The New Culture," *Insight Guide: Russia,* p. 131.

42. Smith, *The New Russians,* p. 151.

CHRONOLOGY

1905
"Bloody Sunday" march in St. Petersburg provokes violent police crackdowns on popular dissent

1917
Czar Nicholas II abdicates, ending the Romanov dynasty; provisional government rules for nine months; Bolshevik Revolution led by Lenin; secret police (Cheka) is formed

1918–1920
Russian civil war between Bolsheviks (Reds) and non-Communist, promonarchist forces (Whites)

1921
New Economic Policy, implemented by Lenin, backs off from communism by permitting private ownership of farms

1924
Death of Lenin; Stalin begins rise to power

1929
Stalin begins forced collectivization of farms; millions of peasants deported or killed

1932–33
Famine kills at least 5 million peasants

1934–1938
Era of Great Purge; millions more killed as suspected "wreckers" of communism

1941
Germany invades Soviet Union, breaking nonaggression pact; Russia joins Allies in World War II

1945
World War II (called Great Patriotic War by Russians) ends; 20 million Russians have died

1953
Stalin dies; rise of Nikita Khrushchev

1956
Khrushchev gives "secret speech" denouncing Stalin; Party faithful are astonished at fall of former idol Stalin

1957
Sputnik launched; nuclear disaster in Kyshtym is covered up

1964
Forced retirement of Khrushchev after embarrassment of Cuban missile crisis and crop failures; rise of Leonid Brezhnev

1968
Czechoslovakian revolt (called Prague Spring) crushed by Red Army

1979
Soviet Union invades Afghanistan

1982
Death of Leonid Brezhnev

1985
Mikhail Gorbachev becomes leader of the Soviet Union

1986
Beginning of glasnost; Chernobyl nuclear disaster

1988
New electoral law establishes multicandidate elections but still permits only one political party

1989
Soviet Union withdraws from Afghanistan

1990
Constitution amended to allow other political parties to form; Baltic republics (Estonia, Latvia, Lithuania) declare independence; Yeltsin resigns from Communist Party

1991
Boris Yeltsin elected president of Russia; unsuccessful coup against Gorbachev; Gorbachev dissolves Communist Party; USSR collapses

1992
"Shock therapy" economic policy begins

1993
Parliament members barricade themselves inside parliament building; Yeltsin orders building shelled and burned to bring them out; new parliamentary election results in rise of Communist and Liberal Democratic Parties; new constitution gives president broader powers

1994–96
War in Chechnya

1996
Yeltsin narrowly wins reelection

1996–1999
Duma and Yeltsin continue struggle over pace of reform

1999
Vladimir Putin appointed, then elected President

GLOSSARY

autonomous: self-governing.

capitalism: economic system characterized by private ownership of and decision making about property and goods, and competition on an open market.

collective: a large holding, such as a farm, put together from many smaller holdings and operated under government supervision.

command economy: economic system in which the central government makes all or most decisions about agricultural and industrial production and business practices.

dacha: a country home.

Duma: the more powerful of the two houses of the Russian Federal Assembly.

federation: An agreement between nations to cede their individual sovereignty to a central authority, but retain a great deal of power to rule themselves.

glasnost: Russian for "openness," referring to new freedoms under Gorbachev.

gulag: a prison camp.

market economy: an economy based on the law of supply and demand and private rather than public decisions about business.

Marxism: A philosophy developed by Karl Marx and Friedrich Engels. Marxism is based on a historical analysis of capitalist societies, claiming that a small upper class has traditionally used its political power to exploit the labor of the poor. Marxists believe that capitalism will eventually fall, to be replaced by a classless society in which the workers themselves, not a wealthy elite, own the businesses, factories and farms, and share the full benefits of their labor.

perestroika: a Russian word for "restructuring" or "reform," referring to Gorbachev's plan to establish a market economy in Russia.

privatization: the process by which formerly state-owned businesses are given to individuals to own and operate.

russification: the process of making Russians of other ethnic backgrounds more like ethnic Russians attempted with limited success.

serf: a person legally bound to a particular piece of land. Distinguished from slavery, which indicates legal bondage to a person, but similar in its effects.

SUGGESTIONS FOR FURTHER READING

BOOKS

James H. Billington, *The Face of Russia: Anguish, Aspiration, and Achievement in Russian Culture.* Washington, DC: TV Books, 1998. Very interesting book focusing on the faces of icons and of people today, with text about Russian arts and society.

Dan Buettner, *Sovietrek: A Journey by Bicycle Across Russia.* Minneapolis: Lerner, 1994. Photographs and journal of the author's 124-day, 7,353-mile bike journey across Russia in 1990.

Zita Dabars, *The Russian Way.* Chicago: Passport Books, 1995. Amusing collection of short articles about the way Russian people live and think. Geared toward tourists who wish to avoid offending Russians, but very interesting reading for anyone.

Kim Brown Fader, *Russia.* Modern Nations series. San Diego: Lucent Books, 1998. Excellent text covering a number of different aspects of Russian history and culture.

John Gillies, *The New Russia.* New York: Dillon Press, 1994. Brief overall picture of life in Russia in the 1990s.

Michael Kort, *Russia.* New York: Facts On File, 1995. Excellent overview of Russian history, culture, and contemporary life.

Shlomo Lambroza, *Boris Yeltsin.* Vero Beach, FL: Rourke Publications, 1993. Clearly written biography with good background on Soviet Union.

Steven Otfinoski, *Boris Yeltsin and the Rebirth of Russia.* Brookfield, CT: Millbrook Press, 1995. Good information about life in and views of present-day Russia.

103

Abraham Remnick, *The Commonwealth of Independent States: Russia and the Other Republics.* Childrens Press, 1993. Good sections on history and overall culture.

Nikolai Popov, ed., *The Russian People Speak: Democracy at the Crossroads.* New York: Syracuse University Press, 1995. Good interviews with a wide variety of contemporary Russians.

Olga Torchinsky, *Cultures of the World: Russia.* New York: Marshall Cavendish, 1994. Brief overview with good pictures and clear information.

William E. Watson, *The Collapse of Communism in the Soviet Union.* Westport CT: Greenwood Press, 1998. Excellent summary and explanation of events. Includes biographical sketches of key political figures and texts of important documents such as Gorbachev's resignation letter.

WEBSITES

CIA World Factbook 1998. www.odci.gov/cia/publications/factbook. Excellent source of up-to-date information about Russia, compiled by the Library of Congress for the Central Intelligence Agency.

Impressions of Russia and the Former USSR. www.cs.toronto.edu. Excellent website with links to major Russian and world news agencies.

WORKS CONSULTED

BOOKS

Deborah Adelman, *The "Children of Perestroika" Come of Age.* New York: M. E. Sharpe, 1994. Thorough study of young people in Russia in the mid-1990s.

John Channon, *The Penguin Historical Atlas of Russia.* London: Penguin Books, 1995. Excellent maps accompanied by short chapters giving clear information about key events in Russian history.

John B. Dunlop, *The Rise of Russia and the Fall of the Soviet Empire.* Princeton, NJ: Princeton University Press, 1993. Scholarly and rather dry treatment of recent Russian history.

Masha Gessen, *Dead Again: The Russian Intelligentsia After Communism.* New York: Verso Books, 1997. Interesting perspective on the future of artists and intellectuals in today's Russia.

Adam Hochschild, *The Unquiet Ghost: Russians Remember Stalin.* New York: Penguin Books USA, 1994. Well-written account of Stalin's legacy of fear, felt to the present day.

Insight Guide: Russia. Singapore: APA Publications, 1998. A good volume in an outstanding series. Provides a wide range of information in one volume, including an excellent historical summary and chapters on Russian lifestyles, in addition to beautiful photographs.

Andrei Kovalev, *Between the Utopias: New Russian Art During and After Perestroika.* Lubbock, TX: Craftsman House, 1996. Good reproductions of art and intelligent text discussing the changes in art since the lifting of constraints on free expression in Russia.

Peter Kurth, *Tsar: The Lost World of Nicholas and Alexandra.* Boston: Madison Press, 1998. Beautiful coffee-table volume containing many large photographs of the czar's family and homes and a text that includes many passages from family members' diaries.

John Morrison, *Boris Yeltsin: From Bolshevik to Democrat.* New York: Penguin, 1991. Thorough biography, but does not include Yeltsin's years as president of the Russian Federation.

Brian Moynahan, *The Russian Century: A History of the Last Hundred Years.* New York: Random House, 1994. Very readable short history of Russia in the twentieth century.

David Remnick, *Lenin's Tomb: The Last Days of the Soviet Empire.* New York: Vintage Books, 1994. A Pulitzer Prize–winning history of the fall of communism by the current editor of the *New Yorker.*

———*Resurrection: The Struggle for a New Russia.* New York: Vintage Books, 1998. A companion volume to *Lenin's Tomb,* that brings the reader up to 1998.

Robert Service, *A History of Twentieth-Century Russia.* Cambridge MA: Harvard University Press, 1997. A very detailed, scholarly approach to recent Russian history.

Hedrick Smith, *The New Russians.* New York: Avon Books, 1990. Very thorough and interesting analysis of the Russian character and experience through 1990. Told through stories of individual Russians and Smith's own experience as a Pulitzer Prize–winning reporter for the *New York Times.*

Leo Tolstoy, *War and Peace.* New York: Signet Books, 1968. Tolstoy's 1869 epic novel about Russia at the time of the invasion by Napoléon.

Daniel Yergin and Thane Gustafson, *Russia 2010—and What It Means for the World.* New York: Vintage Books, 1995. Very readable analysis of possible future paths for Russia, based on today's political and cultural situation.

Boris Yeltsin, *Against the Grain.* New York: Summit Books, 1990. Yeltsin's autobiography, written before he became president of the Russian Federation, discussing his rise to fame and his political perspectives.

Periodicals

Gary Cartwright, "Moscow Makes a Comeback," *National Geographic Explorer,* April 1999.

Andrew Meier, "Russia in the Red," *Harper's Magazine,* June 1999.

Russia Today, "The Constitution of the Russian Federation of Dec. 12, 1993," June 30, 1999. http://www.russiatoday.com.

Websites

Criminal Justice Resources for the Russian Federation. http://arapaho.nsuok.edu. Good source of information about the Russian legal system and government.

Economist Intelligence Unit: Russia. www.eiu.com. Good source of information about economics and other issues affecting the Russian Federation today.

Donald N. Jensen, "How Russia Is Ruled: Continuity of Elites," Radio Free Europe/Radio Liberty, 1998, www.rferl.org. A series of brief articles explaining contemporary Russian politics, by the associate director of broadcasting for Radio Free Europe/Radio Liberty.

INDEX

Picture Credits

About the Author

Laurel Corona lives in Lake Arrowhead, California, and teaches English and humanities at San Diego City College. She holds a master's degree from the University of Chicago and a Ph.D. from the University of California at Davis.